Just North of the Border

By Dave DeWitt and Nancy Gerlach

The Fiery Cuisines
Fiery Appetizers
The Whole Chile Pepper Book

By Dave DeWitt

Texas Monthly Guide to New Mexico
Hot Spots
The Food Lover's Handbook to the Southwest
   (with Mary Jane Wilan)

How to Order:
Quantity discounts are available from the publisher, Prima
Publishing, P.O. Box 1260D&G, Rocklin, CA 95677; telephone (916)
786-0426. On your letterhead include information concerning the in-
tended use of the books and the number of books you wish to
purchase.

Just North
of the
Border

Dave DeWitt & Nancy Gerlach

Prima Publishing
P.O. Box 1260D&G
Rocklin, CA 95677
(916) 786-0426

For Robert Spiegel, who took the risk

Production by Ed Lin, Bookman Productions
Copyediting by Candace Demeduc
Typography by Bookends Typesetting
Interior design by Renee Deprey
Cover design by The Dunlavey Studio
Illustrations by Elizabeth Morales-Denney
Cover photography by John Parrish, © 1991

Portions of this book appeared in *Chile Pepper* magazine. Used by permission.

Library of Congress Cataloging-in-Publication Data
DeWitt, Dave.
    Just north of the border / Dave DeWitt & Nancy Gerlach.
      p. cm.
    Includes index.
    ISBN 1-55958-214-6 (pbk.) : $14.95
    1. Cookery, American—Southwestern style.   I. Gerlach, Nancy.
II. Title.
TX715.2.569D38 1992
641.5979—dc20   92-23039
                            CIP

92 93 94 95 RRD 10 9 8 7 6 5 4 3 2 1

Printed in the United States of America

CONTENTS

PREFACE

As editors of *Chile Pepper* magazine, we are frequently asked what kind of food we cook most often. Well, here it is. Although we regularly taste and test recipes from all over the world, because we live in the Southwest we are greatly influenced by our culinary surroundings. We are fascinated with this regional cuisine which—paradoxically—is both traditional and rapidly evolving.

This is not a beginner's cookbook, so we assume some knowledge on the part of the cooks using it. To explain terms and to suggest substitutions, we have compiled a glossary. Mail order sources for Southwestern ingredients and products are included at the end of the book.

Since we are self-confessed chileheads, most of the recipes in this book contain the pungent pods in some form, except for several breads, drinks, and desserts. Cooks can easily adjust heat levels by simply increasing or decreasing the amount of chiles listed. We hope fellow cooks enjoy these recipes as much as we do. Even if you don't live in the Great Southwest, at least you have the chance to re-create its tastes!

Dave DeWitt and Nancy Gerlach
Albuquerque, New Mexico
Spring 1992

ACKNOWLEDGMENTS

Thanks to the following people who both inspired and helped us: Jennifer Basye, Jane Jordan Browne, Jeff Gerlach, and Mary Jane Wilan.

Just North of the Border

The southern border of this country meanders for 2,000 miles from the Pacific Ocean to the Gulf of Mexico and separates four states—California, Arizona, New Mexico, and Texas—from their most important culinary heritage, Mexico. Although Arizona and New Mexico and parts of Texas and California are in the Southwest and their cookery is called Southwestern cuisine, in reality several distinct yet related cuisines have developed in this vast and divergent region.

Southwestern cooks often claim that the food of their particular state is the most "authentic," a word that is often misused. In fact, there are many versions of authentic Mexican cooking; each is a variation on culinary themes originating in a particular region of Mexico. As travelers to Mexico know, the food served in Mexico City or Puerto Vallarta is quite different from that prepared in Ciudad Juárez, yet each is authentic Mexican cooking in its own right.

When speaking of the cuisines of the Southwest, it is better to drop the word *authentic* from the vocabulary and speak of regional variations as either traditional or new. After all, the term *authentic* implies that any variations from the standard dish are corrupt forms, whereas the word *traditional* innocently indicates that a time-honored method has developed within a certain geographical area.

Within the boundaries of the Southwest, a number of regional cuisines have developed. They are called New Mexican, Tex-Mex, New Southwest, California Mission, and Sonoran-style. Additionally, many Southwestern cities now have Mexican regional restaurants, which influence local chefs and home cooks. Recipes for these various cuisines are included in this cookbook, and where practicable we have included as many variations as possible to illustrate regional differences.

Origins: The Legacy of Old Mexico

Long before Europeans arrived in the New World, ancient peoples settled the two American continents from Alaska to Tierra del Fuego. During the long process of migration and settlement, these peoples developed agriculture in Central and South America independent of the Old World. They based their cookery on four staple foods uniquely American in origin: corn, beans, chile peppers, and squash. These foods—unknown in Europe—were combined with native meats and spices to create a cuisine that caught the European invaders by surprise.

For example, chile peppers were eaten in recipes using every conceivable protein source—mostly venison, fish, and fowl. But when times got tough, the resourceful and iron-stomached Native Americans would consume "frog with green chiles, newt with yellow chiles, tadpoles with small chiles, and lobster with red chiles," as historian Bernardino de Sahagún observed in 1569. Another observer, Francisco Hernandez, noted in 1615 that the native peoples consumed at least seven different kinds of chile peppers.

The arrival of the Spanish in Mexico had a profound effect on the cuisine of the country. They brought with them pigs, cows, sheep, goats, wheat, and vegetables like onions, to name just a few of the foodstuffs that soon transformed the local eating habits. The Aztecs, however, did not give up their beloved staple foods; they combined them with the new imports to create the basis for the Mexican cuisines of today.

Throughout the centuries, an astonishing variety in Mexican cooking developed as a result of geography. From the Yucatán Peninsula, Mexico stretches over two thousand miles to the deserts of the north; so the length and size of Mexico, combined with the fact that mountain ranges separate the various regions, led to the development of isolated pockets of regional cuisines. This is why the cooking of tropical Yucatán differs significantly from that of the deserts of Chihuahua and Sonora.

One common factor, though, in Mexican cookery is the prevalence of chile peppers. They are grown all over Mexico, from the Pacific and Gulf Coasts to mountainous regions with altitudes above eight thousand feet. Approximately two hundred thousand acres of cultivated land produce five hundred thousand tons of fresh pods and thirty thousand tons of dried pods each year. Although dozens of different varieties are grown or collected in Mexico, poblanos, serranos, mirasols, and jalapeños account for seventy-five percent of the crop.

Although chiles are grown and consumed all over Mexico, they are particularly evident in the cooking of northern Mexico, which is termed "Norteño-style" Mexican food, or the food of *La Frontera,* the frontier. In fact, in Mexico City the fiery cooking of the states of Chihuahua and Sonora is termed *platillos nortenses,* or "northern plates." The lore of Mexican cuisine holds that Norteño-style cooking is the hottest of them all—it is this heat that ended up just north of the border.

There are several ways to distinguish one cuisine from another, but the most important is probably the use of different varieties of chile peppers. Since chiles are a common ingredient all over the Southwest, their selection and use is often a clue to the origin of a certain recipe. Another method is to observe the ways a single popular dish (called a "comparison dish") like huevos rancheros is prepared in the various states of the Southwest. Southwest food expert Anne Lindsay Greer adds, "Defining regional differences is like matching food and wine—significant amounts of tasting will educate the palate."

New Mexican Cuisine: Chiles, Chiles, and More Chiles

The interaction of Mexicans, Native Americans, and Americans in the Spanish territory of Nuevo Mexico (literally, "another" Mexico rather than "new" Mexico) produced perhaps the most unique Southwestern cuisine, one that has changed the least over the centuries and depends upon chile peppers more than any other. According to most accounts, chile peppers first were introduced into New Mexico by Capitán General Juan de Oñate, who founded Santa Fe in 1598. But other evidence suggests that New Mexico's Pueblo people may have transferred the fiery pods to the Spanish. Perhaps the Pueblos domesticated their chiles from wild chiltepíns, as did their brothers to the south, or maybe chile pepper seeds were introduced into the Southwest through trade between the Pueblos and the Toltecs and Aztecs.

Because no archaeological evidence exists of chile peppers occurring in the Southwest as early as they did in Mexico, it is more likely that they were introduced from the south, where they grow as perennials. In the colder north, along the Rio Grande, the plants could be cultivated as annuals. From about A.D. 1050, regular trade routes were established between Casas Grandes in Chihuahua and the Rio Grande pueblos, enabling the Pueblos to trade turquoise and salt to the Toltecs for copper, seashells, parrots, and, presumably, dried chiles containing seeds.

Many Pueblo chile recipes have been passed down through the oral tradition, indicating extensive pre-Hispanic culinary usage. After the Spanish began settlement, however, the cultivation of chile peppers exploded—they were grown all over New Mexico. Several different varieties were cultivated, including poblanos, serranos, and jalapeños, but the "long green" chile pepper (now known generically as New Mexican) reigned supreme. This particular variety, which dries bright red, was cultivated with such dedication that several land races (localized varieties) developed in New Mexico. These cultivars, called "Chimayo" and "Española," are still planted today in centuries-old fields. They constitute a small but distinct part of the thirty-six thousand dry tons of chile peppers produced each year in the state.

Most of the primary dishes in New Mexican cuisine contain chile peppers: sauces, salsas, stews, enchiladas, tamales, burritos, carne adovada, huevos rancheros, and many combination vegetable dishes. Other traditional New Mexican ingredients not as common in other parts of the Southwest include blue corn, a type of native corn used in tortillas and corn chips; piñon nuts, which are one of the few crops in the world harvested in the wild rather than cultivated; and posole, corn that has been treated with lime.

New Mexican chile sauces are cooked and pureed, whereas the salsas use fresh ingredients and are uncooked. Debates rage over whether tomatoes should be used in cooked sauces such as red chile sauce for enchiladas. Despite the recipes in numerous cookbooks (none of whose authors live in New Mexico), traditional cooked red and green chile sauces do *not* contain tomatoes. Uncooked salsas, however, usually do. The chile peppers most often used in salsas are serranos or green New Mexican chiles. Our comparison dish, huevos rancheros, is prepared by poaching eggs in red or green chile sauce. The eggs are then placed over softened corn tortillas, covered with more chile sauce, and garnished with fresh tomatoes.

We often think of Southwestern cuisines as being imported from Mexico, but as food writer Jim Peyton points out, "The cooking of New Mexico was not brought across the border by immigrants; the border itself was moved south, leaving the cuisine intact." The American Southwest should be viewed as the northernmost range of Mexican-influenced cookery.

New Mexican cuisine today is a rich mixture of traditions evolved from Native American, Mexican, and American sources, plus variations that reflect the influence of modern restaurant chefs and innovative home cooks. Despite its uniqueness, only recently has it achieved the fame it justly deserves; in the past, the cuisine of New Mexico was overshadowed by the cooking of its huge neighbor to the east.

Tex-Mex Cuisine: Barbecue and Chili Con Carne Reign Supreme

Like New Mexican cuisine, Texas cuisine was influenced mostly by the Norteño-style of cooking, and Texans love their versions of enchiladas and tamales. As Texas food writer Richard West explains, "The standard Tex-Mex foods existed in Mexico before they came here. What Texas restaurant cooks did was to throw them together and label them Combination Dinner, Señorita Dinner, and the hallowed Number One. In so doing, they took a few ethnic liberties and time-saving shortcuts. For example: Tex-Mex tacos as we know them contain ground, instead of shredded, meat."

The chile peppers most commonly used in Tex-Mex cuisine are the poblanos from Mexico, which are tasty, mild, and usually served stuffed with meats or beans; the serranos for fresh salsas; the chilipiquín, (or chiltepín) for soups and stews; and, of course, the ubiquitous jalapeño. This fat and fiery pepper is popular everywhere and is served raw, pickled, stuffed, and chopped in salsas; it even appears in cooked sauces for topping enchiladas and huevos rancheros, which are served Tex-Mex–style with fried eggs and salsa ranchera over corn or wheat tortillas. New Mexican chiles are gradually making an appearance in Tex-Mex cooking, especially in the dried red form.

A fairly recent innovation in Tex-Mex cooking are fajitas, which are prepared with skirt steak (beef diaphragm muscle). Fajitas have their roots in the dish carne asada, thin steaks roasted or grilled until well done. But fajita skirt steak is marinated first in jalapeño juice and port wine. Its name means "little belts," an allusion to the fact that after grilling, the steak is cut across the grain into thin strips. These strips are placed on wheat tortillas and topped with fresh salsa, cheese, tomatoes, and sometimes guacamole.

It is believed that fajitas originated on the vast *ranchos* surrounding Monterrey, Mexico, and gradually worked their way north. In the early 1960s, Sonny "Fajita King" Falcon established the first fajita stand in Kyle, Texas. Twenty years later, the Austin Hyatt-Regency was serving thirteen thousand orders of fajitas a month. Nowadays, fajitas are not limited to skirt steak; they are made from flank and sirloin steaks and variations include chicken and lamb.

Perhaps the most famous Tex-Mex creation is that bowl o' red, chili con carne, a dish that most writers on the subject say did *not* originate in Mexico. Even Mexico disclaims chili; one Mexican dictionary defines it as "a detestable dish sold from Texas to New York City and erroneously described as Mexican."

Despite such protestations, the combination of meat and chile peppers in stewlike concoctions is not uncommon in Mexican cooking. Mexican *caldillos* (thick soups or stews), *moles* (meaning "mixture"), and *adobos* (thick sauces) often resemble chili con carne in both appearance and taste because they all use similar ingredients: various types of chiles combined with meat (usually beef), onions, garlic, cumin, and occasionally tomatoes.

E. De Grolyer, a scholar and chili aficionado, believed that Texas chili con carne had its origins as the "pemmican of the Southwest" in the late 1840s. According to De Grolyer, Texans pounded together dried beef, beef fat, chile peppers, and salt to make trail food for the long ride out to the gold fields and San Francisco. The concentrated, dried mixture was then boiled in pots along the trail as a sort of "instant" chili.

A variation on this theory holds that cowboys invented chili while driving cattle along the lengthy and lonely trails. Supposedly, range cooks planted oregano, chiles, and onions among patches of mesquite to protect them from foraging cattle. The next time they passed along the same trail, they would collect the spices, combine them with beef (what else?), and make a dish called "trail drive chili." Undoubtedly, the chiles used with the earliest incarnations of chili con carne were the chilipiquíns in Texas, which grow wild on bushes, particularly in the southern part of the state.

Probably the most likely explanation for the origin of chili con carne in Texas comes from the heritage of Mexican food combined with the rigors of life on the Texas frontier. Most historians agree that the earliest written description of chili came from J. C. Clopper, who lived near Houston. He wrote of visiting San Antonio in 1828: "When they [poor families of San Antonio] have to pay for their meat in the market, a very little is made to suffice for the family; it is generally cut into a kind of hash with nearly as many peppers as there are pieces of meat—this is all stewed together."

Except for this one quote, which does not mention the dish by name, historians of heat can find no documented evidence of chili in Texas before 1880. Around that time in San Antonio, a municipal market—El Mercado—was operating in Military Plaza. Historian Charles Ramsdell noted that "the first rickety chili stands were set up in this marketplace, with the bowls of red sold by women who were called 'chili queens.'"

The fame of chili con carne began to spread, and the dish soon became a major tourist attraction, making its appearance in Mexican restaurants all over Texas and elsewhere. At the World's Fair in Chicago in 1893, a bowl o' red was available at the San Antonio Chili Stand.

Given the popularity of the dish, some commercialization of it was inevitable. In 1898 William Gebhardt of New Braunfels, Texas, produced the first canned chili con carne, which appeared in San Antonio under the Gebhardt brand, a name still in existence today.

The chili queens were banned from San Antonio in 1937 for health reasons—public officials objected to flies and poorly washed dishes. The stands were restored by Mayor Maury Maverick (his real name) in 1939, only to be closed again shortly after the start of World War II. But Texans have never forgotten their culinary heritage; in 1977 the Texas legislature proclaimed chili con carne the "Official Texas State Dish."

Today chili con carne is enormously popular in Texas and other states, and huge chili cook-offs are held. Teams of cooks use highly secret recipes to compete for thousands of dollars in prizes while having a good old time partying. Some traditionalists, however, scorn the cook-off–style chili con carne as too elaborate and are promoting a return to the classic, "keep it simple, stupid," cafe-style chili.

It should be pointed out that Tex-Mex cuisine is not only Mexico-oriented. It has also been greatly influenced by the basic foods of the East and Midwest, and by Southern cooking—especially barbecue. Texas ranch barbecues are legendary for their huge size, with whole goats and pigs and sides of beef cooked for days over low heat. The differences between grilling and barbecuing are important to remember: Grilling uses high heat and quick cooking; barbecuing is more akin to smoking, using low or indirect heat for a long time. Another important distinction is that barbecue sauces are used to baste barbecued or smoked meats but are generally not placed on grilled meats because their sugar content causes them to burn easily.

Other influences prevail as well in Texas. Along the Gulf Coast, seafood is quite important; although not usually included in the category of Tex-Mex cuisine, fish and shrimp are often combined with jalapeños to create the spiciest seafood dishes imaginable. The closer one gets to Louisiana, the more prevalent are influences from its hot Tabasco and cayenne cuisines. And Texas restaurants have been influenced by yet another force, one which began on the West Coast and has steadily moved eastward.

New Southwest Cuisine: Arizona and California Take the Lead

Although Father Eusebio Francisco Kino introduced cattle, sheep, horses, and wheat into Arizona in 1691, Arizona remained sparsely settled (as compared to New Mexico and Texas) until the arrival of cattlemen and miners during the 1800s. There was no Camino Real connecting the region with Mexico City, so the Spanish influence upon cuisine was not as pervasive, except around Tucson, which was settled by migration from the

Mexican state of Sonora. Early frontier and territorial cookbooks have an abundance of Anglo recipes like sourdough biscuits, rhubarb pie, beef stew, and roast turkey.

The Arizona version of Mexican cooking, often referred to as "Sonoran-style," shows many Native American influences like fry bread and mutton stew. Cactus fruits are commonly used, especially saguaro and prickly pear. One aboriginal Pima recipe calls for cholla cactus buds with green chile, and a traditional Navajo meal uses chicos (dried roasted corn) in a stew with lamb and red chiles.

Generally speaking, Arizona cuisine is not as fiery as that of New Mexico or Texas; the chiles used most are mild New Mexican varieties, and many Sonoran recipes call for no chiles at all. Mexican poblanos and dried anchos are surprisingly uncommon. These general rules are often contradicted when the fiery chiltepín enters the picture. This progenitor of the modern chile pepper grows wild in Sonora and southern Arizona on perennial bushes, as in Texas. The red, berrylike pods are harvested, dried, and crushed, and then sprinkled over soups, stews, and salsas.

However, as is true for the entire country, jalapeños and the hotter New Mexican varieties are steadily invading both Arizona and California. Growers are increasing the size of fields and more of the fiery fruits are being imported from New Mexico. In Arizona our comparison dish, huevos rancheros, is surprisingly served Texas-style, with fried eggs on top of wheat or corn tortillas smothered in a mild chile sauce that often contains tomatoes.

In the westernmost part of the Southwest, wheat tortillas are more popular than corn, primarily because farmers in both Sonora and Arizona grow more wheat than corn. These tortillas are usually quite large—as much as sixteen inches across—and when stuffed with meat, beans, and cheese are called "burros," which are more popular than enchiladas.

Perhaps the most famous Arizona specialty dish is the chimichanga, whose name is translatable only as "thing-a-ma-jig." It is a burro (usually stuffed with beans or ground meat, chiles, and cheese) that is deep-fried and served with guacamole and a pico de gallo–type salsa.

Similar styles of Southwestern cuisine prevail in Southern California, where Mexican cooking is often termed "California Mission" because it originated in the missions of the Spanish padres. It has been influenced by California's abundance of fruits, vegetables, and seafood. The chiles used most often here are Anaheims, a California variety of a New Mexican chile. Mexican poblanos also make their appearance, especially in New Southwest dishes. Goat cheeses, similar to traditional Mexican asadero, are used in enchiladas and to stuff mild chiles; tomatillos, avocados, and fresh cilantro are also widely used.

Coauthor Nancy Gerlach moved from California to New Mexico in the early 1970s and remembers the differences in cuisines. The only chiles used in California cooking were the large, mild Anaheims or occasionally jalapeños in salsas; dried red chiles were rarely used, and tomatoes were usually added to both salsas and sauces in Mission cooking. She was surprised not only by the amount of red chiles used in New Mexico but also by the greatly increased heat levels.

Like most Southwestern cuisines, California's has been influenced by people other than Mexicans, particularly Americans during the Gold Rush and Asian peoples like the Chinese and Japanese. The state's Mediterranean climate—and the fruits and vegetables that thrive in it—has led to variations on Italian, French, and Spanish dishes. Especially popular are dates, olives, grapes, figs, oranges, and avocados.

Salads are beloved on the West Coast and are served in every imaginable variation. American food expert Jonathan Leonard has observed: "To my knowledge, California is the only place where truck drivers eat fresh salads with their meals without fear of being considered effete." A recent innovation in salad design has been the addition of grilled meats and poultry, which are topped with spicy, chile-based dressings.

California restaurants have led the way in the development of what is called New Southwest cuisine. Some characteristics of this cooking style are the use of fresh, locally produced ingredients, the elimination of fattening or high-cholesterol ingredients, the regular appearance of more exotic chiles, and a dedication to the beautiful presentation of the meal. New Southwest chefs rarely use canned, frozen, or otherwise prepared foods.

Perhaps the most famous of these restaurants is Chez Panisse, which opened in 1971 in Berkeley and featured Alice Waters' French-California specialties, such as Corn Soup with Roasted Poblano Chiles and Charcoal-Grilled Veal with Mustard Herb Butter. John Sedlar's St. Estephe Restaurant in Manhattan Beach is renowned for its artistic presentation of New Southwest dishes, and the Fourth Street Grill in Berkeley loves chile peppers so much that once a year it features "A Culinary Celebration of the Chile Pepper." This two-week celebration offers all-chile dinners such as Mesquite-Grilled Hawaiian Tuna with Mango, Serrano, and Pineapple Chutney and Chile-Braised Pork with Small Squashes and Flowers.

Gradually, New Southwest cuisine moved east. Arizona has its representative restaurants, such as Vincent's in Phoenix, Janos and Cafe Terra Cotta in Tucson, and the Piñon Grill in Scottsdale. In Texas, Houston's Cafe Annie (which offers Rabbit with Poblano Maple Sauce) and Dallas's Routh Street Cafe (famous for its Roast Tenderloin of Beef with Ancho Chile Tamarind Sauce) are the leaders in New Southwest cuisine.

One California transplant (from Chez Panisse and the Fourth Street Grill), Mark Miller of Santa Fe's Coyote Cafe, creates recipes that epitomize New Southwest cuisine. Formerly an anthropologist, he believes in a sort of culinary evolution, in which cookery must move forward. "Southwestern cuisine today is frozen in time. It neither looks to the past nor progresses into the future. In New Mexico, for instance, the 'traditional' foods can be traced back only a few generations to the Spanish, when in reality the food tradition extends all the way back to the ancient Anasazi culture."

As a culinary anthropologist, Mark is often accused of corrupting traditional foods by preparing such dishes as Wild Mushroom Tamales. "Indigenous cultures cooked with what they found around them," Mark insists. "Tradition in this case means the native larder, and Native Americans consumed both corn and mushrooms. Since we can assume the same level of sophistication occurred in both their pottery and their cookery, wild mushroom tamales are not only traditional, they are logical recreations of what the ancient Southwest Native Americans probably ate."

Although disconcerting to some, the innovations of the New Southwest chefs are fully in keeping with historical tradition—the interaction of various cultures with different ideas of what constitutes Southwestern cookery. In the recipes that follow, cooks may take their choice from a wide variety of Southwestern recipes from all over the region: the traditional, the modified, and the truly innovative.

A Note on Roasting and Peeling New Mexican Chiles

New Mexican chiles are usually blistered and peeled before being used in recipes. Blistering or roasting the chile heats the fresh pods to the point that the tough transparent skin separates from the meat of the chile so it can be removed.

To roast and peel chiles, first cut a small slit in the chile close to the stem end so that the steam can escape and the pod won't explode. Our favorite roasting method, which involves meditation with a six-pack of Santa Fe Pale Ale, is to place the pods on a charcoal grill about five to six inches from the coals. Blisters will soon indicate that the skin is separating, but be sure that the chiles are blistered all over or they will not peel properly. Although the chiles may burn slightly, take care that they do not blacken too much or they will be difficult to peel.

Immediately wrap the chiles in damp paper towels and place them in a plastic bag to steam for ten to fifteen minutes. During the peeling process, the best way to avoid chile burns is to wear rubber gloves. Remove the skin, stem, and seeds of each pod and chop it coarsely. Either use immediately or place the chopped chile in plastic ice cube trays and freeze it solid. Pop the cubes out, place them in freezer bags, and you'll have easy access to whatever amount of chile you need for a recipe (figure about two cubes equal one chile). The taste of New Mexico will keep in your freezer for at least a year.

2

Aperitivos Are Cocktails and *Finger Food*

In other parts of the country, they are called "appetizers" or "hors d'oeuvre," but in the Southwest the word is *aperitivo*. It refers to anything served before the main courses—snacks or drinks. Here is a collection of some of our favorite cocktails, drinks, and finger foods.

THE PERFECT MARGARITA

Contrary to popular belief, the perfect margarita is made not with Triple Sec but with Cointreau. Also necessary for the perfect margarita are a great tequila and Mexican limes (also called Key limes) rather than Persian limes.

½ **Mexican lime**   1½ **ounces white tequila**
    coarse salt   ¾   **ounce Cointreau**

Squeeze the lime into a shaker full of ice cubes. Next, rub the lime around the lip of an iced cocktail glass and dip the lip into the coarse salt. Add the tequila and Cointreau, shake well, and strain into the cocktail glass.
      Variations: The margarita can also be served on the rocks or blended with ice to make a frozen margarita.

Serves: 1

BLOODY MARIA

Think this drink is just a Bloody Mary with tequila switched for the vodka? Well, almost. *!Salud!*

2 **ounces tequila**   **dash salt**
3 **ounces tomato juice**   1½ **teaspoons bottled chipotle**
¼ **ounce lime juice**   **hot sauce or Habanero Hot**
    dash Worcestershire sauce   **Sauce (see recipe, p. 51)**
    dash celery salt   **slice of lime for garnish**
    dash black pepper

Combine all ingredients and pour over ice. Garnish with a slice of lime and serve with Marinated *Rajas* (see recipe, p. 19).

Serves: 1
Heat Scale: Medium

TEQUILA SUNRISE

Here is another quintessential Southwestern drink. This one was immortalized in song by the rock group the Eagles.

crushed ice
2 ounces tequila
¼ ounce grenadine

3 ounces freshly squeezed orange juice

Fill a tall glass with crushed ice, add the tequila and grenadine, and fill with the orange juice. Stir.

Variation: Use 2 ounces of orange juice and 1 ounce of sparkling water.

Serves: 1

〰〰〰〰〰〰

CHILTEPÍN PEPPER VODKA

The Russians are the true inventors of pepper vodka, which they usually flavor with cayenne. Any type of small fresh or dried chile pepper that will fit in the bottle will work. Be sure to taste the liquor often so you can remove the chiles when it reaches the desired heat—the longer you leave the chiles in, the hotter the vodka will get!

4–6 dried chiltepín chiles,
   left whole

1 quart vodka

Place the chiles in the vodka and let them steep for a week or more. Periodically taste the vodka. Remove the chiles when it is hot enough.

Serving Suggestions: Serve over ice or in tomato juice for an "instant" Bloody Mary.

Note: This recipe requires advance preparation.

Yield: 1 quart
Heat Scale: Medium to Hot

SANGRITA WITH THREE JUICES

Serve as a chaser to straight tequila in a glass rimmed with salt. Sip the tequila, then the sangrita, then suck on a lime slice. Repeat the procedure as often as you dare! Or mix the tequila into the sangrita.

3 green New Mexican chiles, roasted, peeled, stems and seeds removed, chopped
3 cups tomato juice
1 cup orange juice

¼ cup lime juice
2 tablespoons chopped onions
1 teaspoon sugar
salt to taste

Place all the ingredients in a blender and puree until smooth. Chill before serving.

Yield: 1 quart
Heat Scale: Medium

SPICY LAMB CARNITAS

Serve these "little pieces of meat" with toothpicks and several salsas for dipping, such as guacamole (see recipe, pp. 21–22) or other selections from Chapter 4.

1 tablespoon ground red New Mexican chile
3 cloves garlic, minced
¼ cup minced onions
2 teaspoons finely chopped fresh cilantro
1 teaspoon dried oregano

1 teaspoon freshly ground black pepper
1 teaspoon ground cumin
½ teaspoon salt
1 pound boneless lamb, cut into 1- to 1½-inch cubes

Combine all the ingredients except the lamb and rub the meat cubes with the mixture. Allow the meat to sit at room temperature for an hour or more to marinate.

Place the meat on a rack over a pan to catch the drippings. Bake the meat at 250 degrees for an hour or until the meat is crisp on the outside but tender on the inside.

Serves: 6
Heat Scale: Mild

~~~~~~~~~~~~~~~

QUESADILLAS WITH GOAT CHEESE

These tortas are excellent when served as an appetizer, or they can replace sandwiches for a real Southwestern lunch.

6 **8-inch flour tortillas**
8 **ounces goat cheese, crumbled or sliced**
6 **green New Mexican chiles, roasted, peeled, stems and seeds removed, cut into strips**
1 **cup nopales strips**

1 **small avocado, peeled, pitted, and diced**
½ **cup chopped onions**
1 **tablespoon chopped fresh herbs, such as cilantro, oregano, or basil**
  ground red New Mexican chile

On one-half of a tortilla, layer some of the cheese, chiles, nopales, avocado, onions, and herbs. Moisten the edges, fold the tortilla over, and press to seal. Repeat 5 more times.

Toast the tortillas on each side on a hot griddle until the cheese melts. Dust with the ground red chile.

Cut each quesadilla into 4 wedges and serve.

Variation: 4 ounces feta and ¼ cup ricotta cheese may be substituted for the goat cheese.

Yield: 24 wedges
Heat Scale: Medium

EL PASO NACHOS

This appetizer has become so popular that you don't have to travel to Texas to enjoy it, although the nachos you buy outside the Southwest may bear little resemblance to the real thing. Try making your own tostadas, or corn chips, from slightly stale corn tortillas for a more authentic, tasty dish.

1 dozen corn tortillas, cut into wedges
vegetable oil for frying
¾ cup refried beans
½ pound grated sharp cheddar cheese

½ cup sour cream
8 jalapeño chiles, stems and seeds removed, sliced in thin rings

Fry the tortillas in 1½ inches of the oil at 350 degrees until crispy. Remove the drain.

Arrange the tortillas on a pan or oven-proof plate. Place a small amount of beans on each chip and top with the grated cheese. Heat the pan under the broiler until the cheese melts, or microwave the plate for 3 to 4 minutes.

Top with the sour cream and jalapeño slices and serve immediately.

Serves: 6 to 8
Heat Scale: Medium

FRESHLY FRIED NACHOS
WITH CHILE CON QUESO ASADERO

Here is a California version of the Tex-Mex favorite—nachos with, of all things, green olives.

1 dozen corn tortillas, cut into wedges vegetable oil for frying	1 cup finely diced tomatoes
	¼ cup sliced jalapeño chiles, seeds and stems removed
1–1½ cups grated asadero cheese	¼ cup sliced stuffed green olives

Fry the tortillas in 1½ inches of the oil at 350 degrees until crispy. Remove and drain.

Arrange the tortillas on a pan or oven-proof plate. Top with the cheese, tomatoes, chiles, and olives. Heat the pan under the broiler until the cheese melts, or microwave the plate for 3 to 4 minutes.

Variations: Prepare with Monterey Jack or provolone cheese.

Serves: 6 to 8
Heat Scale: Medium

MARINATED *RAJAS*

Rajas, or strips of green chile, are commonly cooked with other vegetables. But New Mexican chiles have such great taste that the *rajas* can stand alone. Serve these tasty appetizers with toothpicks.

5 green New Mexican chiles, roasted, peeled, seeds and stems removed, cut into strips	¼ cup olive oil
	¼ cup red wine vinegar
	1 clove garlic, chopped fine

Combine all ingredients and marinate in the refrigerator overnight.

Note: This recipe requires advance preparation.

Serves: 10
Heat Scale: Mild to Medium

〰〰〰〰〰〰〰〰

JICAMA SLICES WITH
CHOICE OF PEPPERS

The heat of this appetizer will depend on the type of ground chile selected for dipping. And don't limit yourself to jicama—try slices of other fruits and vegetables as well.

1–1½ **pounds jicama, peeled**
⅓   **cup fresh lime juice**
½   **cup salt**

1 **tablespoon each ground chile de árbol, pasilla, and red New Mexican chile**

Cut the jicama into sticks ½ inch wide and 3 to 4 inches long. Pour the lime juice over the sticks, making sure that they are well coated.

Divide the salt into thirds and mix each type of ground chile with one portion of salt.

To serve, arrange the vegetable sticks on a plate with the three chile salts. Guests dip the sticks into the chile salt of their choice.

Serves: 6 to 8
Heat Scale: Mild to Medium

THREE VERSIONS OF GUACAMOLE

The combination of avocados and chiles to form a versatile salsa is common throughout the Southwest. Here are the three best versions. Serve them as a dip with chips, as a salad dressing over greens, as a dipping sauce with roasted meats and poultry, or as a garnish over enchiladas, tostadas, or tacos.

NEW MEXICO VERSION

3 green New Mexican chiles, roasted, peeled, stems and seeds removed, chopped fine

1 tomato, chopped fine

3 medium avocados, pitted, peeled, and mashed

1 medium onion, chopped fine

1 teaspoon lemon juice

¼ teaspoon garlic powder

¼ teaspoon powdered cumin
   salt to taste

Combine all the ingredients and mix well.

Yield: 2 cups
Heat Scale: Mild

TEXAS VERSION

3 jalapeño or serrano chiles, stems and seeds removed, chopped fine

3 medium avocados, pitted, peeled, and mashed

1 medium onion, chopped fine

¼ teaspoon garlic salt
   juice of 1 lemon
   salt to taste

Combine all the ingredients and mix well.

Yield: 2 cups
Heat Scale: Medium

CALIFORNIA VERSION

2   green New Mexican chiles,
     roasted, peeled, stems and
     seeds removed, chopped
3   medium avocados, pitted,
     peeled, and mashed
⅓   cup sour cream

1   small tomato, diced
1   small onion, minced
1   clove garlic, minced
2   teaspoons lemon juice
     salt to taste

Combine all the ingredients and mix well.

Yield: 2 cups
Heat Scale: Mild

〰〰〰〰〰〰〰

GREEN CHILE TORTILLA PINWHEELS

This is an all-purpose filling that goes well on crackers and finger sandwiches. Thin with milk or light cream to make a super dip for chips or
vegetable crudités.

½   cup chopped green New Mex-
     ican chiles, roasted, peeled,
     seeds and stems removed
1   3-ounce package "light"
     cream cheese, softened

2   tablespoons milk or cream
¼   teaspoon garlic salt
2   teaspoons chopped cilantro
3–4 flour tortillas

Combine all the ingredients except the tortillas and mix well.
     Wrap the tortillas in a damp towel and place in a warm oven to
soften. Spread the cream cheese mixture on the tortillas and roll each
tortilla as you would a jelly roll. Slice each roll into rounds ½ inch thick.

Yield: 48 to 60
Heat Scale: Medium

TEXAS MEATBALLS

No hors d'oeuvre table would be complete without some type of cocktail meatballs. These are more like *albóndigas*, or Latin American meatballs, than those of Swedish origin. Serve hot with toothpicks for utensils.

THE MEATBALLS

8 serrano or jalapeño chiles, stems and seeds removed, chopped
1 pound ground beef
1 small onion, chopped

½ cup fresh bread crumbs
2 eggs, beaten
35–40 stuffed green olives
vegetable oil for frying

Combine all the ingredients except the olives. Shape some of the meat mixture around each olive to make a ball.

Saute the meatballs in small batches in the oil until browned. Add more oil if necessary. Remove and drain.

THE SAUCE

1 small onion, chopped
2 cloves garlic, chopped
2 tablespoons vegetable oil
2 tablespoons ground red New Mexican chile

1 cup beef bouillon
1 cup red wine
2 tablespoons cornstarch
2 tablespoons water

Saute the onion and garlic in the oil until soft. Add the chile and cook for an additional minute. Place the onion mixture in a blender with the bouillon and puree until smooth.

Deglaze the pan with the wine. Add the onion puree and simmer until heated. Add more broth, if needed, to make a sauce.

Pour the sauce over the meatballs. Cover and simmer for 15 to 20 minutes to cook the meatballs. Remove the meatballs.

Combine the cornstarch and water. Bring the sauce to a boil and slowly stir in the cornstarch to slightly thicken the sauce.

Pour over the meatballs and serve hot.

Yield: 35 to 40
Heat Scale: Medium

FIESTA BEAN DIP

Pinto beans get their name from the Spanish word for "painted," which refers to the mottled colors of the bean. One of the most popular of the New World beans, they are used in a wide variety of dishes throughout the Southwest. This dip goes well with corn or tortilla chips and can also be used as a filling for burritos or on a tostada.

3 cups cooked mashed pinto beans

6 green New Mexican chiles, roasted, peeled, stems and seeds removed, chopped

2 small tomatoes, peeled and chopped

1 small onion, chopped

½ teaspoon garlic powder

1 cup grated cheddar or Monterey Jack cheese

In a saucepan, heat the beans until very hot. Add all the other ingredients and stir until the cheese melts. Add water, if necessary, to thin to the desired consistency for dipping.

Yield: 3 to 3½ cups
Heat Scale: Medium

QUESO *FLAMEADO* WITH POBLANO STRIPS

This appetizer is so quick and easy to prepare that you can wait until your guests arrive before starting it. It is from the northern states of Mexico but is often served in the Southwest.

2 poblano chiles, roasted, peeled, stems and seeds removed, cut into strips

2 tablespoons butter or olive oil

2 cups grated queso blanco, Monterey Jack, or cheddar cheese

corn tortillas or tostadas for dipping

Saute the poblano strips in the oil until they are soft. In a small casserole dish, add half the cheese, then half the poblano strips, then the remaining cheese. Cover and bake at 300 degrees for about 5 minutes, until the cheese has melted. Uncover, add the remaining strips, and bake for 2 more minutes.

Serve directly from the casserole. Diners scoop out the mixture with tortillas or tostadas.

Serves: 6
Heat Scale: Mild

3

Not Your Ordinary Salad

Compared to other Southwestern dishes, salads are a fairly recent innovation because they depend upon the availability of fresh garden greens and vegetables. The trend these days is to add some ingredients, such as strips of meat and various forms of chile peppers, to create salads unheard of a few decades ago.

SANTA FE GREENS WITH
GREEN CHILE MAYONNAISE

If piñon nuts are not available, substitute sunflower seeds or chopped walnuts in this spicy tossed green salad.

THE DRESSING

4–6 green New Mexican chiles, roasted, peeled, stems and seeds removed, chopped
¼ cup mayonnaise
2 tablespoons sour cream
1 tablespoon olive oil

1 tablespoon lime juice
1 clove garlic, minced
¼ teaspoon sugar
1 teaspoon chopped fresh cilantro
¼ teaspoon ground cumin

Combine all the ingredients and allow the dressing to sit a few hours to blend the flavors.

THE SALAD

½ cup jicama, diced
4 green onions, chopped, including the green part

mixed salad greens— radicchio, butter, red leaf lettuce
¼ cup piñon nuts

Combine the jicama, onions, and salad greens. Toss with the dressing, top with the nuts, and serve.

Serves: 4 to 6
Heat Scale: Medium

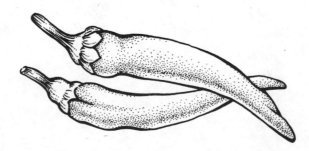

THE DRESSING
This is an optional dressing for the Sonoran-Style Taco Salad and is served on the side.

¼ cup commercial taco sauce

¼ cup red wine vinegar

¼ cup salad oil

2 tablespoons lemon juice

Mix all the ingredients together and allow to sit for a few hours to blend the flavors.

Yield: 1 cup
Heat Scale: Mild

AVOCADO MOUSSE

Prepare this gelatin salad in a fancy mold and garnish it with a side of green chile mayonnaise used in the recipe for Santa Fe Greens (see recipe, p. 28).

1 package unflavored gelatin

1 cup chicken broth

3 small avocados, pitted, peeled, and mashed

3 teaspoons commercial Louisiana hot sauce

2 tablespoons finely chopped onion

2 tablespoons lemon juice

2 tablespoons finely chopped fresh cilantro

½ cup mayonnaise

1 cup heavy cream

Soak the gelatin in ½ cup of the broth. Heat the remaining broth to boiling, stir in the gelatin mixture, and cool in the refrigerator until it starts to thicken.

Place the avocados, hot sauce, onion, lemon juice, and cilantro in a blender and puree until smooth. Mix in the mayonnaise.

Whip the cream until it forms soft peaks.

Combine the avocado and gelatin mixtures. Gently fold the mixture into the whipped cream, pour into a lightly oiled mold, and refrigerate until set.

Serves: 6
Heat Scale: Mild

~~~~~~~~~~~~~~~~~

SOUTHWESTERN CRAB LOUIS

This recipe combines Southern California's devotion to salads and seafood and the ever-growing desire to spice up recipes with green chile.

THE DRESSING

4 green New Mexican chiles, roasted, peeled, stems and seeds removed, chopped

2 tablespoons Classic Red Chile Sauce (see recipe, p. 46)

½ cup mayonnaise

2 tablespoons lime juice, fresh preferred

2 teaspoons prepared horseradish sauce

Combine all the ingredients and let sit for an hour or more to blend the flavors.

THE SALAD

mixed salad greens— butter, romaine, bibb lettuce

1 small onion, thinly sliced and separated into rings

¾ pound cooked crabmeat

black olives for garnish

1 large tomato, cut into wedges

2 hard-boiled eggs, cut into wedges

1 lime, cut into wedges

Arrange the salad greens on plates and top with the onion rings. Mound the crab on top and garnish with the olives. Arrange the tomato, egg, and lime wedges around the salad and serve with the dressing on the side.

Serves: 4
Heat Scale: Medium

wwwwwwwwww

SALPICÓN

It is generally believed that salads with meat or poultry originated with New Southwest cuisine, but this hot and tasty import from Mexico began appearing on El Paso restaurant menus in the late 1940s and is now a local favorite.

2 **pounds beef brisket**	½ **cup vegetable oil**
2 **cloves garlic, minced**	½ **cup wine vinegar**
salt to taste	4 **chipotle chiles in *adobo*,**
1 **cup diced white cheddar or**	**minced**
Monterey Jack cheese	**lettuce leaves**
½ **cup chopped fresh cilantro**	**diced avocado for garnish**
½ **cup diced tomatoes, seeds**	
removed	

Bring the brisket to a boil in water to cover, with the garlic and salt. Reduce heat and simmer for about 1½ hours, uncovered, until the meat is tender and can be shredded. Cool the meat in the broth and then shred finely by hand. Toss the shredded brisket with the remaining ingredients, except the lettuce and avocado. Chill the mixture and allow it to marinate for several hours or preferably overnight.

To serve, line salad plates with lettuce, place the salpicón on top, and garnish with the avocado.

Note: This recipe requires advance preparation.

Serves: 6
Heat Scale: Medium

TEXAS CAVIAR

No collection of dishes from the Southwest would be complete without a recipe for black-eyed peas—or "Texas caviar"—a major crop in eastern Texas. Black-eyed peas are traditionally served on New Year's Day for good luck both in Texas and throughout the South.

6 jalapeño chiles, stems and seeds removed, chopped	freshly ground black pepper
½ cup olive or vegetable oil	2 cups cooked black-eyed peas
¼ cup vinegar	4 green onions, sliced, including the greens
2 cloves garlic, minced	1 stalk celery, chopped
¼ teaspoon dry mustard	

Combine the chiles, oil, vinegar, garlic, mustard, and black pepper to form a dressing. Toss the peas, onions, and celery with the dressing and marinate in the refrigerator overnight.

Note: This recipe requires advance preparation.

Serves: 4 to 6
Heat Scale: Hot

HOT WILTED SPINACH SALAD

The spinach "wilts" when the dressing is poured over it, so be sure the dressing is hot. For a less hearty salad, omit the cheese and nuts.

4 slices bacon, chopped	1 medium red onion, thinly sliced
2 tablespoons crushed red New Mexican chile, seeds included	1 cup cauliflower florets
½ cup cider vinegar	1 cup diced queso blanco or mozzarella cheese
1 tablespoon soy sauce	¼ cup slivered almonds
4 cups fresh spinach	

Saute the bacon pieces until crisp, remove, and drain. Add the crushed red chile to the bacon drippings and saute for a few more minutes.

Mix together the vinegar and soy sauce.

Combine the spinach, onion, cauliflower, and cheese. Toss with the vinegar mixture.

Reheat the bacon fat and chile mixture, pour over the spinach, and toss well. Top with the nuts and bacon and serve.

Serves: 6
Heat Scale: Mild

wwwwwwwwwww

SPANISH CALIFORNIA RIPE OLIVE SALAD

This recipe reflects the heritage of California Mission cookery. You will need the largest olives you can find. The other ingredients are mixed together and then stuffed into the olives—it should be almost but not quite a puree.

½ cup or more cottage cheese

1 tablespoon diced pimento

½ teaspoon salt

½ teaspoon ground red New Mexican chile

1 teaspoon minced fresh parsley

24 colossal ripe olives, pits removed

1 clove garlic

1 egg yolk

¼ cup olive oil

¼ cup lemon juice

1 tablespoon red wine vinegar

1 tablespoon sugar

½ teaspoon salt

1 tablespoon chopped green New Mexican chile, roasted, peeled, stems and seeds removed

butter lettuce

Mix the cottage cheese, pimento, salt, ground chile, and parsley together. Stuff the mixture into the olives.

Rub a mixing bowl with the garlic clove and break the egg yolk into the bowl. Whip the yolk with a wire whisk until the yolk is stiff. Slowly add the olive oil and the remaining ingredients, except the lettuce, while stirring continually.

Place the lettuce on a plate and arrange the stuffed olives on the top. Pour the dressing over the salad and serve.

Serves: 4 to 6
Heat Scale: Mild

CHILE CACTUS SALAD

This interesting salad features nopalitos, the fleshy pads of the Opuntia or prickly pear cactus.

THE DRESSING

⅔ cup olive oil

⅓ cup red wine vinegar

2 jalapeño chiles, stems and seeds removed, finely minced

1 clove garlic, finely minced

¼ teaspoon dried oregano

freshly ground black pepper

Combine a small amount of the oil and vinegar. Whisk in the chiles, garlic, oregano, and pepper and beat until smooth. Slowly add a little oil and beat well, then add a little vinegar. Repeat the process until completely blended.

THE SALAD

1 large poblano chile, roasted, peeled, stems and seeds removed, cut in strips

1 15-ounce jar nopales, drained and rinsed

4 small tomatoes, chopped

2 tablespoons chopped fresh cilantro

red leaf lettuce

½ pound goat or feta cheese, crumbled

Combine all the ingredients, toss with only enough dressing to coat, and serve.

Variation: For a more elegant presentation, toss the lettuce with the tomatoes and place on individual plates. Arrange the chile and nopalito strips on the lettuce. Top with the cheese, garnish with the cilantro, and serve with the dressing on the side.

Serves: 4
Heat Scale: Medium

〰〰〰〰〰

STIR-FRY PORK AND AVOCADO SALAD

Meat salads have been gaining in popularity with the introduction of Southeast Asian immigrants in both California and Texas.

2 tablespoons chile oil
2 teaspoons ground chile de árbol or any hot ground chile
½ teaspoon dried oregano
¼ teaspoon ground cumin
   pinch garlic powder
1 pound boneless pork, cut in strips 2 inches long by ¼ inch wide and thick

   mixed lettuce leaves
1 mung bean sprouts
1 small onion, thinly sliced and separated into rings
1 avocado, pitted, peeled, and sliced
   sliced cucumber
2 tablespoons sesame seeds

Heat the oil and saute the ground chile, oregano, cumin, and garlic for a minute. Add the pork and quickly cook for several more minutes until the pork is done but still tender. Remove and drain.

Place the lettuce on plates. Top with the bean sprouts, onion, avocado, and cucumber slices. Arrange the warm pork strips on top, garnish with the sesame seeds, and serve.

Serves: 4
Heat Scale: Medium

MARINATED VEGETABLES WITH SUN-DRIED TOMATOES

This recipe can be used as a base for a variety of appetizers. Try substituting cauliflower or broccoli for the mushrooms or create your own combination.

THE SALAD

½ cup cider vinegar

1 9-ounce package frozen artichoke halves

½ pound fresh mushrooms, stems removed

4 sun-dried tomatoes, packed in oil, drained, cut in thin strips

12 black olives

THE DRESSING

1 tablespoon crushed red chile

⅓ cup olive oil

¼ cup balsamic vinegar juice of 1 medium lemon

3 green onions, chopped, including some of the green

2 cloves garlic, minced

3 teaspoons dried oregano

½ teaspoon dried basil

Bring 1 cup of water and the cider vinegar to a boil, add the artichokes, and immediately remove the pan from the heat. Let stand for 5 minutes, then remove the artichokes, reserving the liquid. Add the mushrooms and simmer for 5 minutes. Remove and drain. Mix together with the tomatoes and olives.

Mix together the dressing and pour over the vegetables. Marinate them overnight before serving.

Note: This recipe requires advance preparation.

Serves: 4 to 6
Heat Scale: Mild

4

Salsas, Sauces, and the Difference Between Them

Salsas and sauces are essential to Southwestern cuisine. They are similar in that each uses chile peppers of one variety or another and contains fresh vegetables commonly grown in the Southwestern states. The difference between them is simple: Salsas are uncooked, sauces are cooked.

THE SALSA WITH SIX NAMES

This blend of hot chiles and fresh garden vegetables is known both north and south of the border as *salsa fria, pico de gallo, salsa cruda, salsa fresca, salsa Méxicana,* and *salsa picante.* No matter what it's called, or what part of the Southwest it's from, the Salsa with Six Names will always triumph over bottled salsas for the dipping of tostadas, as a taco sauce, or as a relish for roasted or grilled meats. The key to proper preparation is to *never* use a food processor or blender. A marvelous consistency will be achieved by taking the time to chop or mince every ingredient by hand.

6 serrano or jalapeño chiles, stems and seeds removed, chopped very fine

1 large onion, chopped very fine

2 medium tomatoes, chopped very fine

2 cloves garlic, minced

¼ cup finely chopped fresh cilantro

2 tablespoons vegetable oil

2 tablespoons (or less to taste) red wine vinegar or lime juice

Mix all the ingredients together in a nonmetallic bowl. Let stand at room temperature for at least 1 hour before serving.

Serve with tortilla chips as a dip. This salsa is also good with tacos, burritos, and fajitas.

Yield: 2 cups
Heat Scale: Medium

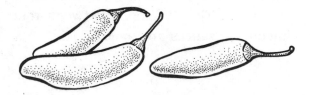

SERRANO SALSA WITH MANGOES AND TOMATILLOS

Not all Southwest salsas are tomato based; this one uses tomatillos, the small "husk tomatoes" that are grown mostly in Mexico but are available fresh or canned in many U.S. supermarkets. The natural sweetness of the mango blends perfectly with the tartness of the tomatillos.

6 red serrano chiles, stems and seeds removed, minced

1 clove garlic, minced

2 tablespoons chopped green onions, including the greens

1 mango, pitted and coarsely chopped

6 tomatillos, husks removed, chopped

½ cup chopped fresh cilantro juice of 1 lime

2 tablespoons olive oil

Combine all ingredients and allow to sit for at least 3 hours—and preferably overnight—to blend the flavors.

Note: This recipe requires advance preparation.

Serves: 4
Heat Scale: Medium

~~~~~~~~~~~~~~~~~~~~~~

SALSA *BORRACHA HERRADURA*

Translated as "drunken horseshoe salsa," this excellent concoction takes its name from one of the finest tequilas made in Mexico—Herradura. This salsa can be used as a marinade for grilled or barbecued meats or poultry as well as an accompaniment to them.

6 serrano chiles *en escabeche,* rinsed, stems removed, chopped
2 tablespoons vegetable oil
1 large onion, chopped
3 cloves garlic, minced
¼ cup lime juice
¼ cup water
¼ cup tequila, Herradura preferred
¼ teaspoon ground cloves

Combine all the ingredients in a blender and puree until smooth.

Yield: 1 cup
Heat Scale: Medium

~~~~~~~~~~~~~~~~

AVOCADO CORN SALSA
WITH FOUR CHILES

Here is an example of a colorful, hearty salsa that can be served either as an accompaniment for grilled meats or atop greens for an interesting and colorful salad.

2 yellow wax chiles, stems and seeds removed, minced
2 red serrano chiles, stems and seeds removed, minced
1 green New Mexican chile, stem and seeds removed, minced
1 orange Habanero chile, stem and seeds removed, minced
1 cup cooked corn
1 cup diced avocado
1 small tomato, diced
1 teaspoon chopped fresh cilantro
1 teaspoon chopped green onions
1 teaspoon chopped red bell pepper
1 teaspoon chopped purple bell pepper
1 teaspoon chopped yellow bell pepper
1 tablespoon lime juice
1 tablespoon olive oil

Combine all ingredients and mix gently. Serve immediately.

Yield: 3 cups
Heat Scale: Medium

~~~~~~~~~~~~~~~~~~~~

ROASTED SERRANO AND
TOMATO SALSA

Of course, there has to be an exception to the rule that salsas are un-cooked and sauces cooked. Here's one in between, a simple but tasty salsa that's served in South Texas *norteño* restaurants. The smooth sauce is flecked with tiny bits of the charred chile and tomato skins, which add an interesting taste.

2 **large tomatoes**   ¼ **teaspoon salt**
2 **serrano chiles, stems
   removed**

Grill the tomatoes and chiles by placing them 3 to 6 inches above hot coals. Turn them often until they are soft and the skins are charred.
    Remove the seeds from the chiles and tomatoes. Puree the vegetables in a blender for about 30 seconds, strain, and add the salt.

Yield: ½ cup
Heat Scale: Medium

GRILLED SOUTHWESTERN SALSA

Here's another version of a partially cooked salsa. This all-purpose salsa can be served with tortilla chips, enchiladas, tacos, and as an accompaniment to grilled entrees. It's also sometimes an ingredient in recipes.

6 green New Mexican chiles	2 medium onions
4 jalapeño chiles	3 cloves garlic
2 large tomatoes	¼ cup chopped fresh cilantro
4 tomatillos	

Make a wood or charcoal fire and let it burn down to coals. Place all the ingredients except the cilantro on the grill only a few inches above the coals. Grill the vegetables until the skins burn and pop, turning occasionally.

    Peel the vegetables, removing the stems and seeds from the chiles, and chop coarsely. Add the cilantro, mix well, and serve.

Yield: 1½ cups
Heat Scale: Hot

~~~~~~~~~~~~~~~~~

CONFETTI SALSA

This brightly colored salsa goes well with grilled or barbecued meats and chicken.

5 jalapeño or serrano chiles, stems removed, chopped	1 small red onion, chopped
1 small bell pepper, stem and seeds removed, diced	1 clove garlic, minced
	3 tablespoons olive oil
1 medium tomato, diced	1 tablespoon lime juice
½ cup whole-kernel corn	1 tablespoon finely chopped fresh basil

Combine all the ingredients and allow to sit for several hours before serving.

Yield: 2 cups
Heat Scale: Medium

wwwwwwwwwwwwww

TOMATILLO SAUCE WITH CILANTRO

Although canned tomatillos are called for in this recipe, you can also use fresh ones. If using fresh tomatillos, remove the husks and boil the tomatillos for 15 minutes or until tender.

4–6 serrano or jalapeño chiles, stems and seeds removed, chopped fine	1 small onion, chopped fine
	2 cloves garlic, minced
1 10-ounce can tomatillos, drained and chopped	¼ cup chopped fresh cilantro salt to taste

Combine all the ingredients except the cilantro and salt and simmer for 30 minutes. Stir in the cilantro and the salt to taste. Cook for an additional minute before serving.
    Variation: For a smoother sauce, puree in a blender.

Yield: 1 to 1½ cups
Heat Scale: Medium

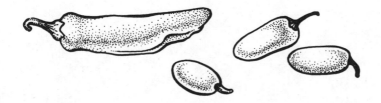

CLASSIC RED CHILE SAUCE, NEW MEXICO–STYLE

This basic sauce can be used in traditional New Mexican or New Southwest versions of beans, tacos, tamales, and enchiladas.

10–12 dried whole red New Mexican chiles	3 cloves garlic, chopped
1 large onion, chopped	3 cups beef broth or water

Place the chiles on a baking pan and place in a 250-degree oven for about 10 to 15 minutes or until the chiles are toasted, taking care not to let them burn. Remove the stems and seeds and crumble the chiles into a saucepan.

Add the remaining ingredients, bring to a boil, reduce the heat, and simmer for 20 to 30 minutes.

Puree the mixture in a blender until smooth, then strain. If the sauce is too thin, place it back on the stove and simmer until it is reduced to the desired consistency.

Variations: Spices such as cumin, coriander, and Mexican oregano may be added. Some versions of this sauce call for the onion and garlic to be sauteed in vegetable oil before the chiles and water are added.

Yield: 2 to 2½ cups
Heat Scale: Medium

CLASSIC GREEN CHILE SAUCE, NEW MEXICO–STYLE

This all-purpose sauce recipe is from the southern part of New Mexico, where green chile is the number-one food crop and is used more commonly than the red form.

1 small onion, chopped
2 cloves garlic, minced
2 tablespoons vegetable oil
6 green New Mexican chiles, roasted, peeled, seeds and stems removed, chopped

1 teaspoon ground cumin
2 cups chicken broth or water

Saute the onion and garlic in 2 tablespoons of oil until soft. Add the chiles, cumin, and water and simmer for ½ hour. The sauce may be pureed in a blender to the desired consistency.

Variations: To thicken the sauce, make a roux by sauteing 1 tablespoon flour in 1 tablespoon vegetable oil, taking care not to let it burn. Slowly stir the roux into the sauce and cook to the desired thickness. Coriander and Mexican oregano may be added to taste. For added heat, add more New Mexican chiles or a serrano or two.

Yield: 2 to 2½ cups
Heat Scale: Medium

PEACHY PECAN SAUCE

Central Texas is hill country, which produces both the pecans and peaches that are used in this recipe. This cooked salsa is an example of a new Southwestern dish that might be served in Austin, accompanying grilled chicken or fish.

½ cup sugar
1 cup orange juice
2 tablespoons vinegar
3 tablespoons crushed dried red New Mexican chile, including the seeds
1 cinnamon stick, 2½ inches long

¼ teaspoon ground cumin
1 tablespoon finely grated orange peel
3 large peaches, pitted, peeled, and chopped
½ cup toasted pecans, chopped

Dissolve the sugar in the orange juice and vinegar. Add the chile, cinnamon, cumin, and orange peel. Bring to a boil, reduce the heat, and simmer for 20 minutes until it becomes a thick syrup. Discard the cinnamon, add the peaches, and simmer for 5 minutes. Stir in the pecans and heat for an additional minute before serving.

Yield: 2 cups
Heat Scale: Mild

¡*OLE MOLE* SAUCE!

Here is our Southwestern version of the classic Mexican sauce that originated in Puebla, Mexico. Here, the traditional lard is replaced with vegetable oil (lard, however, does lend an authentic taste).

4 **dried pasilla chiles, stems and seeds removed (or substitute anchos)**

4 **dried red New Mexican chiles, stems and seeds removed**

1 **medium onion, chopped**

2 **cloves garlic, chopped**

2 **medium tomatoes, peeled and chopped**

3 **tomatillos, chopped**

1 **tablespoon sesame seeds**

1 **tablespoon pumpkin seeds**

½ **cup almonds, chopped**

1 **corn tortilla, torn in pieces**

¼ **cup raisins**

½ **teaspoon oregano**

¼ **teaspoon each ground cloves, cinnamon, and coriander**

3 **tablespoons vegetable oil**

2 **cups chicken broth**

1 **ounce bitter chocolate (or more to taste)**

Simmer the chiles in water for 15 minutes to soften. Remove the chiles and reserve the water.

Combine the chiles, onion, garlic, tomatoes, tomatillos, seeds, almonds, tortilla, raisins, and spices in a blender and puree, in small amounts, until smooth.

Heat the oil in a skillet and saute the puree for 10 minutes, stirring frequently. Add the broth, 1 cup of the chile water, and the chocolate and cook over a very low heat for 30 to 45 minutes, or until thick.

Serving Suggestions: This sauce goes well with any poultry dish and can be used in place of red or green chile sauce for enchiladas.

Yield: 4 cups
Heat Scale: Medium

DEEP, WAY DEEP IN THE HEART
OF TEXAS BARBECUE SAUCE

Until recently, New Mexican chiles were rarely used in Texas cooking. But as the popularity of chili con carne cook-off contests increased, cooks began experimenting with chiles other than the usual chilipiquíns and jalapeños. Here is one result of this broadening of the chile pepper experience.

4	dried red New Mexican chiles, stems and seeds removed	12	ounces beer
4	small dried red chiles such as chilipiquíns or chiltepíns	¼	cup brown sugar
		3	tablespoons cider vinegar
1	large onion, chopped	2	tablespoons Worcestershire sauce
4	cloves garlic, chopped	2	teaspoons dry mustard
2	tablespoons vegetable oil	1	teaspoon freshly ground black pepper
1½	cups catsup		

Simmer the chiles in 1 cup water for 15 minutes or until softened. Puree them in the water to make a smooth sauce. Strain the sauce.

Saute the onion and the garlic in the oil until soft. Combine with the pureed chiles and the remaining ingredients in a saucepan, bring to a boil, reduce the heat, and simmer for an hour.

Puree the sauce until smooth. If it is not thick enough, return it to the heat and continue to simmer until the desired consistency is obtained.

Yield: 2 cups
Heat Scale: Hot

HABANERO HOT SAUCE

Habanero chiles, the hottest in the world, are usually associated with recipes from the Yucatán Peninsula and the Caribbean, but we are seeing more of these bonnet-shaped chiles in the Southwest, especially now that they are being grown in quantity in California and Texas.

½   cup chopped onion
2   cloves garlic, minced
2   tablespoons vegetable oil
6–7 Habanero chiles, stems and
     seeds removed, chopped

¾   cup distilled vinegar
2   tablespoons lime juice
     salt to taste

Saute the onion and garlic in the oil until soft. Add the remaining ingredients, transfer to a blender, and puree the mixture until smooth. Simmer the sauce for 5 minutes to combine the flavors.

Yield: 1 cup
Heat Scale: Extremely Hot

PIMA HOT CHILE RELISH

This is a very old recipe from the Pima tribe of Arizona. It is usually served over eggs or beans but can be served as a side to any Southwestern dish.

1 tablespoon bacon drippings
3 green New Mexican chiles,
   roasted, peeled, stems and
   seeds removed, chopped

½   medium onion, minced
3   large tomatoes, diced
2–4 chiltepíns

Saute the chiles and the onion in the bacon drippings until they become soft. Add the tomatoes and simmer for 5 minutes. Crush the chiltepíns into the mixture and serve.

Yield: 1½ cups
Heat Scale: Medium to Hot

5

A Fine Kettle of Soups and Stews

There are probably more variations on soups and stews than any other type of Southwestern dish. In fact, an entire cookbook could be written on the subject—and probably will be some day. Here are our favorite recipes, which range from traditional to nouveau.

SOPA DE LIMA

This light, delicate soup is easy to prepare and is a great beginning to either lunch or dinner. Freely translated as "lime soup," in Mexico it's made with sour lemons, which are unavailable in this country—but limes are an acceptable substitute.

1   green New Mexican chile, roasted, peeled, stem and seeds removed, chopped
⅓ cup onion, chopped
2   teaspoons vegetable oil
4   cups chicken broth
1   cup cooked, shredded chicken

salt to taste
1   tomato, peeled and chopped
    juice of 1 lime
4   large lime slices for garnish
    tortilla chips for garnish

Saute the chile and onion in the oil until the onion is soft but not browned. Add the chicken broth, chicken, and salt to taste, cover, and simmer 20 minutes. Add the tomato and simmer 5 minutes longer. Stir in the lime juice, taste, and add more if needed.

Serve in bowls garnished with one lime slice and several tortilla chips.

Serves: 4
Heat Scale: Mild

〰〰〰〰〰〰

POSOLE WITH CHILE CARIBE

One of our favorite restaurants in Albuquerque—El Patio—provided this recipe, which is the classic version prepared in northern New Mexico. Serving the chile caribe as a side dish instead of mixing it with the posole allows guests to adjust the heat to their own liking.

cut in 1-inch

antro for

r garnish

heat for about
if necessary.
ntil the pork
e a soup more

owder

ove the pods,
ender, using a
a serving bowl

flour tortillas.
nion in bowls
for garnishes. Each guest can then adjust the pungency of the posole
according to individual taste.

Variation: For really hot chile caribe, add dried red chilipiquíns,
cayenne chiles, or chiles de árbol to the New Mexicans.

Note: This recipe requires advance preparation.

Serves: 4
Heat Scale: Medium to Extremely Hot

CHILE CON QUESO SOUP

The classic combination of cheese and chile appears here as a soup, rather than as a dip or appetizer.

1	medium onion, chopped	2	tomatoes, peeled and chopped
2	tablespoons butter or margarine	1	bell pepper, diced (optional)
3	tablespoons flour	1½	cups half-and-half
3–4	cups chicken broth	8	ounces sharp cheddar cheese, grated
6–8	green New Mexican chiles, roasted, peeled, stems and seeds removed, chopped		

Saute the onion in the butter until soft, then remove the onion.

Add the flour to the butter and cook for 3 minutes, stirring constantly, taking care not to let the flour brown.

Stir in the broth, chiles, tomatoes, and bell pepper and simmer for 30 minutes.

Bring to a boil, reduce the heat, add the half-and-half and the cheese, and heat until the cheese melts and the soup is thickened.

Serves: 4 to 6
Heat Scale: Hot

〰〰〰〰〰〰〰〰〰〰〰

WINTER SQUASH AND APPLE CHOWDER WITH CHILE-DUSTED CROUTONS

This hearty soup combines several of the fall crops from northern New Mexico, namely squash, apples, and both red and green chiles. Add a salad, crusty bread, and a nice New Mexican wine and it's a memorable meal.

CHILE-DUSTED CROUTONS

3 slices of white bread, crusts trimmed, cut in cubes

1 clove garlic, sliced

3 tablespoons butter or margarine

2 teaspoons ground red New Mexican chile

½ teaspoon ground cumin

Spread the bread cubes on a baking sheet and let them dry out at room temperature for 3 hours.

Saute the garlic in the butter for 2 minutes, then remove and discard the garlic. Add the chile and cumin to the butter, then quickly toss the bread until all the cubes are coated with the mixture.

Place the croutons on a cookie sheet in a 350-degree oven for 10 minutes or until they are golden brown.

Note: This recipe requires advance preparation.

THE CHOWDER

1 medium onion, diced

2 tablespoons butter or olive oil

1½ pounds hubbard or butternut squash, peeled, seeded, and cut into 1-inch cubes

3 tart green apples, peeled, cored, and chopped

¼ cup chopped green New Mexican chiles, roasted, peeled, stems and seeds removed

4 cups chicken stock or broth

1 teaspoon grated lemon peel

2 cups diced cooked chicken freshly ground black pepper

2 tablespoons applejack or Calvados salt to taste

1–2 teaspoons cider vinegar (optional)

Saute the onion in the butter until soft. Add the squash and apples and saute for an additional 3 minutes.

Add the chiles and stock and bring to boil. Reduce heat, cover partially, and simmer until the squash and apples are very tender, about 30 to 45 minutes.

Add the lemon peel, chicken, black pepper, applejack, and salt to taste and simmer for an additional 15 minutes. Taste and add the vinegar if the soup is too sweet.

Pour the soup into bowls, top with the croutons, and serve.

Serves: 4 to 6
Heat Scale: Medium

〜〜〜〜〜〜〜〜〜〜

HEARTY CHORIZO AND BEAN SOUP

The spiciness of the chorizo complements the rich flavor of the kidney beans in this easy-to-prepare soup.

1 **pound chorizo, sliced or crumbled**
1 **large onion, chopped**
3 **carrots, diced**
1 **cup chopped celery**
1 **tablespoon crushed red New Mexican chile, seeds included**
2 **cups cooked kidney beans**
2 **tomatoes, peeled and diced**

1 **cup bean water (water that the beans were cooked in)**
3 **cups water or stock**
1 **teaspoon Worcestershire sauce**
1 **teaspoon distilled white vinegar**
½ **teaspoon epazote**
sour cream for garnish

Saute the chorizo to render the fat. Pour off the excess fat, add the onion, carrots, and celery and saute for a few more minutes.

Combine the remaining ingredients except the sour cream and simmer for 30 minutes.

To serve, dish up the soup in individual bowls and garnish with a dollop of sour cream.

Serves: 4 to 6
Heat Scale: Medium

BLACK BEAN SOUP,
SANTA MONICA–STYLE

This rich and creamy soup could almost be a meal in itself. Cru
dough bread and slices of fruit are all you need to make a filling—a
spicy—lunch.

1½ cups black beans, sorted and rinsed clean	1 teaspoon crushed epazote
1 large onion, chopped	1 tablespoon red wine vinegar
2 cloves garlic, minced	7 cups chicken stock
6–8 jalapeño chiles, stems and seeds removed, chopped	½ cup heavy cream or half-and-half
2 tablespoons bacon drippings or vegetable oil	3 tablespoons tequila
1 large ham hock	crushed red chile for garnish
1 teaspoon ground cumin	sour cream for garnish

Cover the beans with water and soak overnight.

Saute the onion, garlic, and jalapeños in the bacon fat until soft.

Combine the sauteed ingredients, beans, ham hock, cumin, epazote, vinegar, and stock, bring to a boil, reduce the heat, and simmer until the beans are soft—about 3 to 3½ hours.

Remove the ham hock, shred the meat, and set aside.

Puree half of the bean mixture until smooth (strain if necessary to obtain desired smoothness). Return to the saucepan containing the remaining beans, stir in the cream, and heat. Remove from the heat and stir in the tequila.

To serve, stir in the shredded ham and garnish with the crushed red chile and a dollop of sour cream.

Variation: Leave all the beans whole for a more robust soup.

Note: *This recipe requires advance preparation.*

Serves: 6 to 8
Heat Scale: Hot

ALBÓNDIGAS MEXICANAS
WITH CRUSHED CHILTEPINS

The heat of this meatball soup comes from the chiltepíns, which are harvested in the wild in Mexico. These little chiles can fool you—they look like red peppercorns but are very, very hot. Leave them whole and remove them before serving so you don't shock your guests.

THE MEATBALLS

3 tablespoons Serrano Salsa (see recipe, p. 41) or your favorite commercial salsa
½ pound ground beef
¼ pound ground pork
¼ cup minced onion

1 egg
½ cup dried bread crumbs
1 tablespoon fresh chopped mint or 1 teaspoon dried mint
2 tablespoons uncooked rice

Combine all the ingredients, adding just enough salsa to hold the meatballs together. Form into walnut-sized balls.

THE SOUP

1 quart beef stock
1 teaspoon whole dried red chiltepíns
2 carrots, thinly sliced

1 stalk celery, thinly sliced
1 small zucchini, thinly sliced
   chopped cilantro or parsley for garnish

Bring the beef stock and chiltepíns to a rolling boil and slowly drop in the meatballs so that the stock does not stop boiling. Skim off any foam that forms. Reduce the heat, cover, and simmer for 20 minutes.

Add the carrots and celery and simmer for an additional 15 to 20 minutes. Add the zucchini and simmer until the vegetables are done but still firm.

Remove the chiltepíns, sprinkle with the chopped cilantro, and serve.

Serves: 6
Heat Scale: Hot

CREAM OF JALAPEÑO SOUP
WITH SHREDDED CHICKEN

Here is another innocent-looking soup that is hotter than it appears. The combination of chicken and chiles occurs often in all Southwestern cuisines but the use of jalapeños is more prevalent in Texas.

4 jalapeño chiles, stems and seeds removed, chopped
1 3-pound chicken, cut in pieces
1 large onion, chopped
1 stalk celery, chopped
2 carrots, peeled and diced
1 clove garlic, chopped

1 teaspoon ground cumin
1 quart water
2 cups half-and-half
1–2 jalapeños, stems and seeds removed, finely chopped for garnish

Combine the first eight ingredients in a saucepan. Bring to a boil, reduce the heat, cover, and simmer until the chicken starts to fall off the bone. Remove the chicken and reserve the stock. Remove the bones, skin, and fat from the chicken and shred the meat.

Puree the stock and strain the mixture so that it is smooth.

Pour 3 cups of the stock into a large saucepan, add the half-and-half, and heat through.

Add the chicken and heat through. Garnish with the finely chopped jalapeños and serve.

Serves: 6
Heat Scale: Hot

ROUTE 66 SOUP

Supposedly, this soup originated during the Depression, when necessity inspired cooks to use available ingredients imaginatively. A highly nutritious soup, it is inexpensive and easy to prepare.

2 **pounds beef bones, washed**	2 **medium potatoes, peeled and diced**
½ **cup dry pinto beans**	2 **carrots, peeled and diced**
½ **cup black-eyed peas**	1 **clove garlic, minced**
2 **tablespoons crushed red New Mexican chile, seeds included celery leaves**	1 **teaspoon salt**
	1 **bay leaf**
1 **large onion, chopped**	¼ **teaspoon freshly ground black pepper**
¾ **cup chopped celery**	

Cover the bones with water and simmer for an hour, skimming off any foam.

Add the beans, peas, chile, and celery leaves and continue to simmer for 1½ to 2 hours or until the beans are tender without being mushy. Add more water if necessary.

Remove the bones and celery leaves. Pull any remaining meat from the bones and return it to the soup.

Add the remaining ingredients and simmer for 30 to 45 minutes or until the vegetables are done.

Serves: 6
Heat Scale: Mild

ROASTED CORN AND CRAB BISQUE

Roasting the corn gives this soup a distinctive flavor; the addition of crab is a Gulf Coast influence. Serve this bisque as the first course of a special holiday dinner.

3   ears of corn with the husks left on
1   teaspoon crushed chilipiquín or other small hot dried red chile
¼   cup diced bell pepper
½   cup chopped green onions
1   clove garlic, minced
2   tablespoons butter or vegetable oil

1   small potato, peeled and diced
2   cups chicken broth
½   cup white wine
1   cup milk
½   cup cream or half-and-half
½   pound lump crabmeat
    crushed red chile for garnish

Soak the ears of corn in their husks in water for 30 minutes. Roast them by placing the ears on a hot grill and turning often until the corn is tender. Or place them in a 400-degree oven and roast them for 20 minutes. Cut the corn off the cobs.

Saute the chilipiquín, bell pepper, onions, and garlic in the butter until the onions are soft.

Combine the onion mixture, potato, and broth and simmer for 30 minutes or until the potatoes are done. Add the corn, wine, and milk and simmer for 15 minutes. Stir in the cream and heat through.

Gently stir in the crab, taking care that the meat does not break down. Simmer for 3 minutes or until the crab is hot. Garnish with the crushed red chile and serve.

Serves: 4 to 6
Heat Scale: Mild

CHILLED GAZPACHO
WITH CHILES VERDES

This soup, originally from Spain, has been transformed by Southwestern chefs into a chilled dish that is nevertheless heated through with chiles.

½	cup chopped green New Mexican chiles, roasted, peeled, stems and seeds removed	2	large ripe tomatoes, peeled and chopped
¼	cup diced bell pepper	¼	cup chopped red onion
2	cups beef stock	2	stalks celery, chopped
1½	cups tomato juice	1	clove garlic, minced
1–2	tablespoons olive oil	2	teaspoons chopped fresh cilantro
4	tablespoons lime juice		salt to taste
1	tablespoon red wine		diced cucumbers for garnish
			ice cubes for garnish

In batches, combine all the ingredients except the garnishes in a blender and puree until smooth. Chill for at least 3 hours to blend the flavors.

To serve, ladle the soup into chilled bowls, garnish with the chopped cucumbers, and place an ice cube in the center of each bowl.

Note: This recipe requires advance preparation.

Serves: 6
Heat Scale: Medium

GREEN CHILE STEW, BORDER-STYLE

This enormously popular dish is sometimes called *caldillo,* or "little broth." There are probably as many versions of it as there are cooks in the Southwest.

2 pounds pork stew meat, cut in 1- to 1½-inch cubes

2 tablespoons vegetable oil

1 large onion, chopped

1 teaspoon chopped garlic

2 cups chopped green New Mexican chiles, roasted, peeled, stems and seeds removed

2 large tomatoes, peeled and chopped

2 potatoes, peeled and diced

½ teaspoon ground cumin

4 cups water

salt to taste

Brown the pork in the oil. Add the onion and garlic and saute until the onion is soft. Remove the meat and onion mixture and deglaze the pan with a cup of water.

Combine the pan drippings and the rest of the ingredients in a large pot or crockpot, bring to a boil, reduce the heat, and simmer for 2 hours or until the meat is very tender and starts to fall apart.

Serves: 6
Heat Scale: Medium

ORIGINAL SAN ANTONIO CHILI

According to legend, this is one of the chili queens' original recipes. Some changes have been made to accommodate people watching their intake of fat (this chili was traditionally prepared with suet and pork fat).

2 pounds beef shoulder, cut into 1½-inch cubes
1 pound pork shoulder, cut into 1½-inch cubes
   flour for dredging
3 tablespoons vegetable oil
2 medium onions, chopped
6 cloves garlic, minced
1 quart water
2 ancho chiles, stems and seeds removed

4 dried red New Mexican chiles, stems and seeds removed
1 serrano chile, stem and seeds removed, chopped fine
1 tablespoon cumin seeds, freshly ground
2 tablespoons Mexican oregano
   salt to taste

Lightly flour the beef and pork cubes. Quickly cook the meat in the oil, stirring often. Add the onions and garlic and saute until soft. Add the water and simmer for 1 hour.

Soak the anchos and dried New Mexican chiles in hot water for 15 minutes. Puree them in a blender with a little of the water and then strain. Add this sauce to the meat mixture along with the remaining ingredients and simmer for an additional 2 hours.

Serve with cooked beans on the side.

Serves: 6
Heat Scale: Medium

〰〰〰〰〰〰

ARIZONA CHILI CON CARNE

Arizona chili takes advantage of two chiles from south of the border—the pasilla and the chiltepín. Add more chiltepíns to spice up this version, which can be mild (they add heat without changing the flavor).

4 dried red New Mexican chiles, stems and seeds removed

1 pasilla chile, stem and seeds removed

2 pounds beef sirloin, cut into 1-inch cubes
   flour for dredging

¼ cup vegetable oil

1 small onion, chopped

3 cloves garlic, minced

2 teaspoons dried oregano

3 cups beef broth

4 chiltepín chiles

Cover the New Mexican and pasilla chiles with hot water and simmer for 15 minutes or until soft. Place the chiles in a blender along with some of the water in which they were soaking and puree. Strain the sauce.

Dredge the beef cubes with the flour and shake off any excess. Brown the cubes in the oil. Add the onion and garlic and saute for several minutes.

Add the chile puree, oregano, and broth. Bring to a boil, reduce the heat, and simmer for an hour or until the meat is tender. Add more broth if necessary.

Crush the chiltepíns over the chili and simmer for an additional 30 minutes before serving.

Serves: 6
Heat Scale: Mild to Medium

〰〰〰〰〰〰〰〰

CALIFORNIA CHILI CON CARNE

Ground beef and beans are popular ingredients in California chili, which is different from the other Southwestern versions. If beans are served in Texas or Arizona, they are side dishes to be added at the table. And they are *never* served with New Mexican chili!

1	onion, chopped	1	teaspoon ground cumin
3	cloves garlic, minced	1	teaspoon sugar
2	tablespoons bacon drippings	2	cups canned whole tomatoes
2	pounds coarsely ground beef	2	cups beef stock
2	tablespoons ground red New Mexican chile	3	cups cooked pinto beans salt and freshly ground black pepper to taste
1	teaspoon ground cayenne		
½	teaspoon ground paprika	1½	teaspoons masa harina

Saute the onion and garlic in the bacon drippings until softened. Add the beef and ground chile and continue to saute until the meat is well browned. Stir in the cayenne, paprika, cumin, and sugar.

Add the tomatoes and beef stock and simmer for 30 to 45 minutes, stirring often. Add the beans and continue to simmer for an additional 30 minutes. Season with salt and pepper.

To thicken, bring to a boil, stir in the masa harina, and mix well. Simmer for an additional 15 minutes.

Serves: 6
Heat Scale: Mild

~~~~~~~~~~~~~~~~~~

CHIMAYÓ RED CHILE STEW

Chimayó chiles are a locally adapted variety of New Mexican chiles that have been grown primarily in the Española Valley in northern New Mexico for hundreds of years. This variety of chile is difficult to find; however, any type of dried red New Mexican pods will provide excellent results. When you order chili in New Mexico, this is what you will be served.

6–8 dried red New Mexican chiles, stems and seeds removed

2 pounds pork or beef stew meat, cut in 1- to 1½-inch cubes

2 tablespoons vegetable oil

4 cups beef broth
   salt to taste

Place the chiles on a baking sheet in a 250-degree oven and roast for 10 to 15 minutes or until you can smell a toasty chile aroma, taking care not to let them burn. Put the roasted chiles in a saucepan, cover with water, and simmer for 15 minutes to soften. Then puree the chiles with the water in a blender until smooth. Strain the sauce.

Brown the meat in the vegetable oil and remove from the pan. Add 1 cup of the broth to the pan to deglaze it.

Combine all the ingredients in a pan or crockpot, bring to a boil, reduce the heat, and simmer for 2 hours or until the meat is so tender that it starts to fall apart and the stew is thickened.

Variations: Spices like cumin, coriander, and Mexican oregano may be added to taste. Some cooks add 2 or 3 cloves of garlic and/or a medium onion, chopped fine.

Serves: 6

Heat Scale: Medium

CACTUS PORK STEW

This stew goes well with warmed flour tortillas. It also makes a tasty filling for burritos.

1 pound boneless pork, cut into 1-inch cubes
2 tablespoons vegetable oil
1 onion, chopped
2 cloves garlic, minced
4 serrano chiles, stems and seeds removed, chopped
1 cup Tomatillo Sauce (see recipe, p. 45)

½ cup chicken broth
1 teaspoon ground cumin
2 potatoes, peeled and diced
1 jar nopalitos, drained, rinsed, and chopped
chopped fresh cilantro for garnish

Brown the pork in the oil. Add the onion, garlic, and chiles and continue to saute until the onions are soft.

Add the Tomatillo Sauce, broth, cumin, and potatoes. Bring to a boil, reduce the heat, and simmer for 45 minutes to an hour or until the potatoes are done and the meat is tender, adding more broth if necessary.

Add the nopalitos and simmer for an additional 5 minutes.

Garnish with the chopped cilantro and serve.

Serves: 4
Heat Scale: Medium

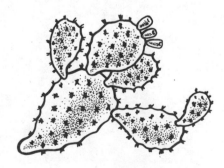

Meaty Matters

Before the arrival of the Spanish in the Southwest, Native American cooks used deer, rabbit, and peccary in their recipes. Nowadays, the selection of meats is far greater, with beef, pork, and lamb preferred in both traditional and new dishes. However, game has made a comeback because of its availability and is now frequently prepared.

CHILE-ROASTED ROSEMARY LEG OF LAMB

Here is an entree that is both dramatic and elegant. The lamb is carved at the table and served with twice-baked potatoes and a colorful vegetable, such as dilled whole baby carrots.

8–10	green New Mexican chiles, roasted, peeled, stems removed, chopped		flour for dredging seasoned with ground red New Mexican chile, salt, and pepper to taste
2	cups chopped leeks	1	large carrot, chopped
½	cup chopped fresh rosemary	1	large onion, chopped
8	cloves garlic, coarsely chopped	1	large potato, peeled and chopped
4	tablespoons butter or margarine	1½	cups water
1	4-pound leg of lamb, boned and butterflied	2	cups dry red wine
		3	tablespoons flour
		½	cup milk

Preheat the oven to 450 degrees.

Saute the chiles, leeks, rosemary, and garlic in the butter until the leeks are soft. Spread the mixture on the lamb, roll it up, and tie the roast in 4 to 6 places to hold it together. Lightly dust the roast with the seasoned flour.

Place the carrot, onion, and potato in the bottom of a roasting pan with 1½ cups water.

Place the roast on a rack in a roasting pan above the vegetables, immediately reduce the heat to 350 degrees, and roast the lamb to desired doneness, usually 20 minutes per pound for rare.

Remove the lamb and keep warm. Discard the vegetables and deglaze the pan with the wine, stirring constantly, then strain. Place the drippings in a saucepan and bring to a boil. Combine the flour and milk and slowly stir into the drippings to form a thick sauce.

Carve the lamb into slices, pour the wine sauce over them, and serve.

Serves: 8
Heat Scale: Mild

GRILLED PIÑON LAMB CHOPS

Here is a delicious combination of ingredients from the Southwest—piñons, chile, and lamb. For an authentic, smoky flavor, grill the chops over mesquite wood or charcoal covered with mesquite chips soaked in water.

1 tablespoon ground red New Mexican chile
¾ cup olive oil
5 tablespoons roasted piñon or pine nuts
½ cup tomato paste
¼ cup vinegar
3 cloves garlic
4 lamb chops, 1 to 1½ inches thick

Combine all the ingredients except the lamb in a blender and puree until smooth. Paint the chops with the mixture and allow them to marinate for at least an hour.

Grill the chops, turning them occasionally until done, about 7 to 10 minutes per side.

Serves: 4
Heat Scale: Mild

SAUTEED LAMB CHOPS WITH CHIMAYÓ RED WINE SAUCE

The following recipe combines wine with chile to produce a spicy sauce. Many aficionados say that Chimayó chile is the most flavorful of the New Mexican red chiles, but if it is not available, substitute any ground red chile.

4 teaspoons ground red New
  Mexican chile, Chimayó
  preferred
2 teaspoons finely chopped
  fresh cilantro
2 teaspoons ground oregano
1 teaspoon ground cumin
1 teaspoon garlic powder

4 large, thick lamb chops
3 tablespoons vegetable oil
4 tablespoons chopped onion
1 clove garlic, minced
½ cup beef broth
1 cup dry red wine
2 tablespoons butter

Combine 1 teaspoon of the chile with the cilantro, oregano, cumin, and garlic powder and rub the mixture into the lamb chops. Marinate the meat for an hour or more.

Heat 2 tablespoons of the oil in a heavy skillet until very hot. Saute the lamb for a few minutes on each side or until medium rare. Remove and keep warm.

Add the remaining oil, remaining ground chile, and the onion and garlic. Quickly saute until the onion starts to brown.

Increase the heat to high, add the broth, bring to a boil, and deglaze the pan. Add the wine, reduce the heat, and simmer for 15 to 20 minutes or until the sauce is reduced by half. Remove, strain, and stir in the butter.

To serve, place the lamb chops on a plate and top with the sauce. Serve any remaining sauce on the side.

Serves: 4
Heat Scale: Medium

NEW MEXICO CARNE ADOVADA

This variation of an ancient recipe evolved from the need to preserve meat before refrigeration. The red chile acts as an antioxidant to prevent the meat from spoiling. Such technical details should not detract from the fact that this simple dish is incredibly tasty—and once eaten is never forgotten.

1½ cups crushed red New
    Mexican chiles, stems
    removed, seeds included
4   cloves garlic, minced
1   teaspoon dried oregano

3 cups water
2 pounds pork, cut into strips
2 medium potatoes, peeled and
  chopped
2 onions, chopped

Combine the chiles, garlic, and oregano in a saucepan. Add the water and heat for 5 minutes to make a coarse chile sauce.

Place the pork in a glass dish, cover the meat with the chile sauce, and let it marinate for 12 to 24 hours in the refrigerator, turning it once or twice.

Add the potatoes and onions to the pork and chile and bake in a 300-degree oven for 2 hours or until the pork is very tender and starts to fall apart.

Serving Suggestions: Place the adovada mixture in a flour tortilla, top with grated cheese, and eat as a burrito. Use it as a stuffing for sopaipillas or as a filling for enchiladas.

Note: This recipe requires advance preparation.

Serves: 6
Heat Scale: Hot

SMOKED PORK *MOLE* ENCHILADAS

Serve these unusual enchiladas with a chilled citrus salad, rice pilaf, and a seasoned green vegetable dish from Chapter 10.

2 ancho chiles, stems and seeds removed
2 pasilla chiles, stems and seeds removed
3 dried red New Mexican chiles, stems and seeds removed
3 cups water
2 cups chicken broth

1 large onion, chopped
1 pork roast, 4–6 pounds
1 dozen corn tortillas
2 tablespoons vegetable oil
8 ounces sour cream
¼ cup sesame seed
Mole Sauce (see recipe, p. 49)

Simmer the chiles in the water for 15 minutes to soften. Drain the chiles and puree them with the chicken broth and onion in a blender until smooth. Strain the sauce if desired.

Make diagonal slits about 1 inch deep in the pork roast. Rub the chile mixture over the roast, being sure it goes deep into the cuts.

Smoke the roast in a smoker with indirect heat, following the directions provided by the manufacturer (smoking approximately 1 hour per pound). When the roast is done, carve it into thin strips.

Soften the tortillas by frying them in the oil for a few seconds on each side, then drain them on paper towels. Place the pork strips in the tortillas, top with sour cream and some sesame seeds, and roll up. Place them in a baking dish, cover with the *mole* sauce, and bake in a 325-degree oven for about 20 minutes. Sprinkle the remaining sesame seeds on top and serve.

Serves: 6 to 8
Heat Scale: Medium

PORK CHORIZO

This traditional Mexican sausage is often served with huevos rancheros for breakfast. Unlike other sausages, it is usually not placed in a casing but rather served loose or formed into patties.

1 **clove garlic**	½ **teaspoon salt**
½ **cup ground red New Mexican chile**	1 **teaspoon oregano**
½ **teaspoon freshly ground black pepper**	½ **cup vinegar**
¼ **teaspoon each ground cloves, cinnamon, oregano, cumin**	2 **pounds ground pork**

Combine all the ingredients except the pork in a blender and puree. Knead this mixture into the pork until it is thoroughly mixed together. Cover and refrigerate for 24 hours. At this point the chorizo may be frozen.

    To cook, crumble the chorizo in a skillet and fry. Drain it before serving.

    Note: This recipe requires advance preparation.

Serves: 8
Heat Scale: Medium

〰〰〰〰〰〰〰〰〰

TAMALES *Y MAS* TAMALES

Tamales can be filled with almost anything from meat or poultry to fruits and nuts. To create variations on this traditional recipe, simply replace the pork with the ingredients of choice. For example, many of the meat and poultry entrees in this cookbook could be used instead.

2 **pounds pork bones**
Classic Green Chile Sauce (see recipe, p. 47)
dried corn husks
4 **cups masa harina**
1 **teaspoon salt**

2½–3 **cups broth or water**
⅔ **cup lard or shortening**
Avocado Corn Salsa with Four Chiles (see recipe, p. 42)

In a large pot, cover the pork with water, bring to a boil, reduce the heat, and simmer for an hour or until the pork is very tender and starts to fall apart. Remove the roast and save the broth. With fingers or 2 forks, finely shred the meat.

Combine the pork with 1 cup of the green chile sauce and simmer for 15 minutes, adding more sauce if the meat becomes too dry.

Soak the corn husks in water to soften.

Mix together the masa harina and salt. Slowly add the reserved pork broth, stirring with a fork until the mixture holds together. Whip the lard or shortening until fluffy. Add the masa harina to the shortening and continue to beat. Drop a teaspoonful of dough into a glass of cold water. If the masa floats, it is ready. If it sinks, continue to beat it until it floats.

To assemble, select corn husks that measure about 5 by 8 inches or overlap smaller ones together. Place 2 tablespoons of masa in the center of the husk and pat or spread the dough evenly into a 2-by-3-inch rectangle. Place about 3 teaspoons each of the pork and the Avocado Corn Salsa down the center. Fold the husk around the masa and filling, being careful not to squeeze the tamale.

There are two basic ways of securing the corn husks. The first is to use two strips of husk to firmly tie each end of the tamale. This method works well with smaller husks.

The second method is to fold the tapered end over the filled husk and then fold the remaining end over it. Tie the tamale around the middle with a strip of husk to keep the ends folded down.

Place a rack in the bottom of a steamer or large pot. Make sure that the rack is high enough to keep the tamales above the water. Place the tamales on the rack, folded side down; if the pot is large enough, stand them up. Do not pack them tightly because they need to expand as they cook. Cover with additional husks or a towel to absorb the moisture.

Bring the water to a boil, reduce to a gentle boil, and steam for an hour for each dozen tamales or until done. To test for doneness, open one end of a husk; if the masa pulls away from the wrapper, the tamale is done.

Serving Suggestions: Serve with additional Classic Green Chile Sauce on the side.

Yield: 2 dozen
Heat Scale: Medium

~~~~~~~~~~~~~~~~~~~~

PORK CHOPS RANCHEROS

The addition of cumin and chiles gives these pork chops a wonderful Southwestern flavor.

6 green New Mexican chiles, roasted, peeled, stems and seeds removed, chopped	2 cloves garlic, minced
	2 teaspoons ground cumin
¼ cup lime juice	1 teaspoon dried oregano
2 tablespoons vegetable oil	½ teaspoon ground coriander
¼ cup chopped onions	½ teaspoon salt
	4 thick-cut pork chops

Combine all the ingredients except the pork. Marinate the pork in the mixture for 4 hours or overnight

Remove the chops from the marinade and grill until done.

Serving Suggestions: The remaining marinade can be heated and served on the side as a sauce.

Note: This recipe requires advance preparation.

Serves: 4
Heat Scale: Medium

SOUTHWESTERN SPICY PORK PAELLA WITH ARTICHOKES

Paella, one of the most famous one-dish meals, was born in Valencia, Spain. Traditionally made with seafood and/or chicken, there are also countless variations using a wide variety of ingredients, as in the following recipe.

¾ pound boneless pork, cut in 1-inch cubes
3 tablespoons olive oil
2 chorizo sausages, cut in thin slices or crumbled
1 medium onion, chopped fine
4 cloves garlic, chopped fine
1 tablespoon crushed red New Mexican chile, including the seeds

2 cups long-grain rice
¼ teaspoon saffron mixed with ¼ cup chicken stock
1 large tomato, peeled and chopped fine
4 cups chicken stock
1 14-ounce can artichoke hearts, drained and quartered
½ cup cooked green peas

Brown the pork in the oil. Add the chorizo, onion, garlic, and chile and saute until the onion is soft. Remove the pork and chorizo and reserve. Add the rice and continue to saute until the rice starts to turn golden.

Stir in the saffron mixture, tomato, and stock and remove from the heat. Transfer to a baking dish and arrange the pork, chorizo, artichoke hearts, and peas over the top. Bake at 400 degrees for 30 to 45 minutes or until the rice is done.

Remove the dish from the oven, remove the lid, and drape a kitchen towel loosely over the top. Let it sit for 5 to 8 minutes before serving.

Serves: 6
Heat Scale: Mild

BRISKET OF BEEF AUSTIN-STYLE

Brisket, one of the tastiest cuts of beef, needs marinating and slow cooking to achieve perfect flavor. The key to cooking the brisket is to keep the moisture in by sealing the pan and holding the cooking temperature below the boiling point of water. Leftover brisket makes great sandwiches.

6   jalapeño chiles, stems and seeds removed, chopped
½   cup vegetable oil
¼   cup dry red wine
¼   cup soy sauce
1   large onion, finely chopped
4   cloves garlic, minced

2   tablespoons lime juice
2   tablespoons tequila
1   tablespoon coarsely ground black pepper
1   teaspoon ground cumin
3   pounds beef brisket
1   cup water

Combine all the ingredients except the beef and water. Marinate the brisket in the mixture in a nonmetallic pan for 12 to 24 hours, turning two or three times.

Place the brisket, the marinade, and the water in a baking dish. Cover and bake in a 200-degree oven for 3 hours (or more) until the brisket starts to fall apart.

Remove the brisket. Transfer the marinade and juices to a saucepan and reduce until thick.

Slice the brisket across the grain into thin pieces. Serve the sauce over the brisket slices.

Serving Suggestions: Brisket is great with coleslaw (see recipe, p. 29) and a baked potato or Texas Jalapeño Onion Rings (see recipe, p. 138).

Note: This recipe requires advance preparation.

Serves: 6
Heat Scale: Medium

JALAPEÑO-STUFFED STEAKS

Nowadays grilled steaks are often more than simply a piece of plain meat, as this recipe shows. Any type of fresh chile or combination of chiles can be substituted for the jalapeños in this dish. The stuffing can be prepared a day in advance and refrigerated. An hour before cooking, slice the steaks and fill with the chile mixture.

10	jalapeño chiles, stems removed, chopped	½	cup grated Monterey Jack cheese
1	medium onion, chopped	3	pounds trimmed fillet of beef, cut into 6 thick steaks
4	cloves garlic, chopped		freshly ground black pepper
1	tablespoon vegetable oil		

Saute the chiles, onion, and garlic in the oil for several minutes, until barely soft (they should still be a little crisp). Remove, cool, and stir in the cheese.

Slice into the steaks horizontally, creating a "pocket" for the stuffing. Stuff with the jalapeño mixture and fasten the opening with a toothpick if necessary. Season the outside of each steak with the black pepper.

Grill over hot charcoal to the desired doneness.

Serves: 6

Heat Scale: Hot

SOFT *MACHACA* AVOCADO TACOS

The use of shredded beef in these tacos instead of ground beef reflects the more traditional Mexican influences. Besides, it is much more tasty.

8 **chilipiquíns or chiltepíns, crushed**
1 **pound boneless beef roast, cut up**
2 **small onions, chopped**
2 **cloves garlic, sliced**
8 **corn tortillas**
1 **tablespoon vegetable oil**
2 **poblano chiles, roasted, peeled, stems and seeds removed, chopped**

2 **medium tomatoes, chopped**
2 **teaspoons dried oregano**
¼ **teaspoon ground cumin**
   diced avocados or guacamole (see recipe, pp. 21–22) for garnish
   chopped cilantro for garnish
   Salsa with Six Names (see recipe, p. 40)

Place the chilipiquíns, beef, one-half the onion, and the garlic in a pan with enough water to cover. Bring to a boil, reduce the heat, and simmer covered for 1 hour or until the meat starts to fall apart.

Remove the meat, allow to cool, and shred the meat by using two forks.

Wrap the tortillas in a damp towel and warm them in a 300-degree oven.

Saute the remaining onions in the oil until soft. Add the chopped poblanos, tomatoes, oregano, and cumin and saute for 5 minutes. Add the meat and cook until thoroughly heated.

Place the meat in the warmed tortillas and add the avocados or guacamole and chopped cilantro as garnishes. Serve the salsa on the side.

Serves: 4
Heat Scale: Medium

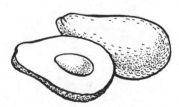

BARBECUED RIBS, TEXAS-STYLE

The Texas Panhandle is beef country and was once the scene of cattle drives through such cities as Amarillo and Abilene. Texans love to barbecue beef, which can take hours or even days, but the results are worth it. The following recipe doesn't take twenty-four hours, but the ribs should be cooked slowly over charcoal, taking care that the sauce doesn't burn.

6	jalapeño chiles, stems and seeds removed, chopped	1	tablespoon mustard
1	medium onion, chopped	1	tablespoon brown sugar
3	cloves garlic, chopped	½	teaspoon dried oregano
2	tablespoons vegetable oil	⅛	teaspoon ground Habanero chile
1	cup tomato sauce		freshly ground black pepper
2	cups beef broth	3	pounds spareribs
¼	cup cider vinegar		
	juice of 1 lemon		

Saute the jalapeños, onion, and garlic in the oil until soft. Place the mixture in a blender and puree until smooth.

Add the remaining ingredients except the ribs and bring to a boil. Reduce the heat and simmer until the sauce has thickened enough to hold its shape.

Grill the ribs about 6 inches from the coals until browned, about 30 to 45 minutes. Baste the ribs with the sauce and continue to baste every 10 minutes for an additional 30 minutes, being careful that they do not burn.

Remove and serve.

Serves: 4 to 6
Heat Scale: Hot

TOURNEDOS CHIPOTLE

We confess to smuggling Mexican recipes into the Southwest. Here is the preferred way to prepare steaks in Puerto Vallarta, a method we fell completely in love with during visits there.

4 beef fillets, 1–2 inches thick olive oil	½ teaspoon oregano
	½ teaspoon sugar
1 onion, chopped	½ teaspoon freshly ground
3 cloves garlic, minced	black pepper
2 tablespoons vegetable oil	2 cups beef broth
3 canned chipotle chiles in *adobo*	1 cup dry red wine
1 medium tomato, peeled and seeds removed, chopped	

Brush the steaks with olive oil and let sit while preparing the sauce.

Saute the onion and garlic in the vegetable oil until browned. Add the chipotles, tomato, oregano, sugar, and pepper and saute for several more minutes. Stir in the broth and wine and simmer for 20 to 30 minutes or until reduced by a half.

Remove from the heat and puree in a blender until smooth. Strain, return to the pan, and keep warm until ready to serve.

Broil or grill the steaks to desired doneness.

To serve, place some of the sauce on a plate, place the steak on top of the sauce, and top with additional sauce.

Serves: 4
Heat Scale: Hot

ARIZONA BEEF JERKY

Preserving meat by drying has always been popular throughout the Southwest where the hot dry weather speeds up the process. Jerky, or *carne seca*, can be used in burritos and enchiladas, with scrambled eggs, and substituted for the beef in Soft *Machaca* Avocado Tacos (see recipe, p. 83).

2 **pounds extra-lean beef sirloin or flank steak**	1 **teaspoon crushed chiltepíns**
4 **cloves garlic, cut in half**	1 **teaspoon ground cumin**
2 **tablespoons lime juice**	**coarse salt**
4 **tablespoons ground red New Mexican chile powder**	**freshly ground black pepper**

Rub the beef with the garlic cloves. Cut the meat across the grain in slices ⅛ inch thick and 1 inch wide. If you are having difficulty, partially freeze the meat before cutting.

Combine the remaining ingredients and rub the strips with the mixture.

Place the strips on a rack over a drip pan in the oven. Bake at 150 degrees, turning several times, for 6 to 8 hours or until the meat is very dry. Leaving the door to the oven slightly ajar will help speed up the drying process.

Note: This recipe requires advance preparation.

Yield: Approximately 1 pound
Heat Scale: Hot

FAJITA FEAST

Typically Texan, these recipes make a great outdoor barbecue party. They are easy to prepare; simply marinate them the night before and grill them when the guests arrive.

CHICKEN FAJITAS

½ cup canned jalapeño chiles, chopped fine
½ cup chicken broth
⅓ cup lemon juice
⅓ cup vegetable oil

1 teaspoon ground cumin
1 teaspoon oregano
¼ teaspoon garlic powder
½ can beer
3 chicken breasts

BEEF FAJITAS

½ cup chopped serrano chiles, stems removed
⅓ cup lime juice
⅓ cup soy sauce

⅓ cup red wine
2 tablespoons vegetable oil
2 cloves garlic, minced
2 pounds skirt or flank steak

Combine the ingredients for each marinade and marinate the chicken and beef separately for 12 to 24 hours.

Grill the meats over mesquite wood or charcoal and mesquite chips to desired doneness. Carve the steak diagonally against the grain in thin strips as for London broil. Cut the chicken breasts in thin strips.

Serve with flour tortillas, chopped onions, grated cheese, sour cream, diced avocados, and a variety of sauces and salsas from Chapter 4. The idea is for each guest to custom-make their own fajita sandwiches.

Serving Suggestions: Serve with a crisp tossed salad or Tex-Mex Coleslaw (see recipe, p. 29), beans, and Jalapeño-Cheddar Blue Corn bread (see recipe, p. 145).

Note: This recipe requires advance preparation.

Serves: 8
Heat Scale: Medium

Firebirds of a Feather

Southwestern poultry dishes illustrate the diversity of preparation methods used in the region: roasting, smoking, grilling, and in combination with other ingredients—especially corn and chile peppers. Substitutions are encouraged in these recipes: for example, duck for chicken and pheasant for quail.

ROASTED SAGUARO JAM–GLAZED GAME HENS WITH CORN BREAD, PIÑON, AND GREEN CHILE STUFFING

Here is a good example of some of the substitutions that can be made in these poultry recipes. In place of saguaro cactus jam, try prickly pear jam or even jalapeño jelly. The stuffing can be used in roasted chicken or turkey, and the Cornish hens can be replaced with duck or chicken.

2 tablespoons butter or margarine
1 small onion, chopped
4 green New Mexican chiles, roasted, peeled, stems and seeds removed, chopped
½ cup celery, chopped
3 cups corn bread, coarsely crumbled

½ cup roasted piñon nuts
1 teaspoon each fresh thyme and sage, chopped
½ cup chicken broth
4 Cornish game hens
1 cup saguaro cactus jam sauces and/or salsas from Chapter 4

Melt the butter in a saucepan and saute the onion until soft. Combine the onion, chiles, celery, corn bread, piñons, and herbs and mix thoroughly. Add enough broth to moisten but not saturate the mixture, and mix well.

Stuff the hens with the mixture and close the opening. Spread the jam over the hens and roast in a 350-degree oven for 1 hour, basting with additional jam.

Carefully cut each hen in half to expose the stuffing and serve with more jam, warmed, on the side, along with several sauces or salsas from Chapter 4.

Serves: 4
Heat Scale: Mild

CHICKEN, CHILE, AND CHEESE CHIMICHANGAS

These fruit-sweetened chimichangas are lighter than the more traditional beef and bean recipe popular in Arizona.

1 medium onion, chopped fine	6 flour tortillas
1 tablespoon vegetable oil	1 cup grated Monterey Jack cheese
4 green New Mexican chiles, roasted, peeled, stems and seeds removed, chopped	vegetable oil for deep-fat frying
3 cups cooked diced chicken	chopped lettuce and tomato for garnish
½ teaspoon ground cinnamon	salsa (recipe from Chapter 4)
¼ teaspoon ground cloves	
1 small orange, peeled, seeded, and chopped	

Saute the onion in the oil until soft. Add the chiles, chicken, and spices and saute for an additional 5 minutes. Add the chopped oranges and mix well.

Wrap the tortillas in a moist towel and place them in a warm oven to soften. Place approximately ½ cup of the mixture in the center of each tortilla and top with cheese. Fold the tortilla like an envelope and secure with a toothpick.

Deep-fry the chimichangas, one at a time, in 375-degree oil until well browned. Drain on paper towels and remove the toothpick.

Serve topped with the chopped lettuce and tomato and a salsa from Chapter 4.

Serves: 6
Heat Scale: Mild

MARGARITA-MARINATED GAME HENS

This is a recipe for people who would rather eat their margarita than drink it. You can either bake the hens or split them and cook on a grill, basting with the marinade.

4–5	serrano chiles, stems and seeds removed	2	teaspoons sugar
½	cup lime juice	1	teaspoon chopped fresh cilantro
¼	cup vegetable oil	4	Cornish game hens
2	tablespoons tequila		

Combine all the ingredients except the hens in a blender and puree. Pour the mixture over the hens and marinate for 2 hours at room temperature or overnight in the refrigerator.

Place the hens in a 450-degree oven and immediately reduce the heat to 350. Roast for 30 to 45 minutes or until done, basting often with the marinade.

Note: This recipe requires advance preparation.

Serves: 4
Heat Scale: Medium

〜〜〜〜〜〜〜〜

TOMATILLO-CHICKEN ENCHILADAS WITH TWO KINDS OF GREEN CHILES

Southwestern cooks are forever improvising on traditional recipes. This interesting variation on green chile and chicken enchiladas has been tested so many times in our kitchens that we now consider it a New Southwest classic.

4 **chicken breasts**
8 **ounces cream cheese**
1 **cup onions, chopped fine**
1 **cup heavy cream or half-and-half**
3 **green serrano chiles, stems and seeds removed, chopped fine**
5 **green New Mexican chiles, roasted, peeled, seeds and stems removed, chopped**

1 **cup toma**
 removed,
 chopped
¼ **cup chop**
½ **teaspoon**
 black pe
1 **egg**
 vegetable oil for frying tortillas
12 **corn tortillas**

Cover the chicken with water, bring to a boil, reduce the heat, and simmer 30 minutes. Remove the chicken and reserve the stock. When the chicken has cooled, remove the skin and bones and shred the meat using two forks.

Combine the cream cheese, onions, and ¼ cup of the cream. Add the chicken and mix well.

Place the serranos, green chiles, tomatillos, cilantro, pepper, egg, remainder of the cream, and ⅓ cup of the reserved stock in a blender and puree to make a smooth sauce.

Heat 2 inches of oil in a pan until hot. Fry each tortilla for a few seconds on each side until soft, taking care that they do not become crisp. Remove and drain.

To assemble the enchiladas, dip a tortilla into the green sauce and place it in a shallow casserole dish. Spread about ¼ cup of the chicken mixture in the center of the tortilla, roll it up, and place it in the dish with the folded side down. Repeat the process until the enchiladas form a single layer in the dish, then pour the remaining sauce over them.

Bake the enchiladas uncovered in a 350-degree oven for 20 minutes and serve immediately.

Serving Suggestions: The enchiladas go well with traditional dishes of rice, refried beans, and a crisp garden salad.

Serves: 6
Heat Scale: Medium

SMOKED TURKEY WITH CASCABEL OIL

This simple dish yields a complex taste. Serve the turkey hot with the chile oil and a salsa on the side, or cold on a Chile-Dusted Cheese *Bolillo* from Chapter 11.

½ cup vegetable oil	2 teaspoons dried oregano
6 cascabel chiles, stems and seeds removed, crushed	salt and freshly ground black pepper
4 cloves garlic, chopped	1 10-pound turkey

Heat the oil and saute the chiles and garlic until softened. Remove from the heat and add the oregano, salt, and pepper.

Split the turkey in half by cutting through the breast and backbone. Brush the chile oil over the turkey and marinate for 2 hours at room temperature.

Place the turkey sections, breast side up, on a grill in a smoker. Smoke with indirect heat over an aromatic wood like pecan, apple, or hickory. Baste the turkey with the oil every half-hour until the turkey sections are done, approximately 4 hours.

Serves: 6 or more

Heat Scale: Mild

STUFFED CHICKEN BREASTS WITH WALNUT *PIPIAN*

The Mayans are credited with creating *pipians*, sauces that are both flavored and thickened with seeds and/or nuts. In this recipe, the *pipian* also adds color to the dish.

THE CHICKEN

3 chicken breasts, skinned, bones removed, cut in half

6 green New Mexican chiles, roasted, peeled, stems and seeds removed, left whole

6 thin slices ham

6 slices asadero or Monterey Jack cheese

1 large avocado, peeled and sliced

3 tablespoons chopped fresh cilantro

¼ cup melted margarine

Pound the chicken breasts until thin. Top each piece of chicken with a chile, a slice of ham, a slice of cheese, and some avocado and cilantro. Roll each piece tightly and place folded side down in an oven-proof dish. Brush with the margarine, cover, and bake for 45 minutes at 325 degrees. Remove the cover and continue to bake until the top is golden brown.

THE SAUCE

1 medium onion, chopped

1 clove garlic, chopped

1 poblano chile, roasted, peeled, stem and seeds removed, chopped

4 tablespoons margarine or vegetable oil

½ cup chopped walnuts

¼ cup freshly chopped cilantro

2 cups chicken broth
walnut pieces for garnish

To make the sauce, saute the onion, garlic, and chile in the margarine or vegetable oil until the onion starts to brown. Place this mixture and the walnuts and cilantro in a blender and puree until smooth, using a little broth to thin if necessary.

Return to the saucepan, stir in the broth, and simmer for 20 to 30 minutes until thickened.

To serve, place the chicken on a plate, pour the sauce over the top, and garnish with a few chopped walnut pieces.

Serves: 4 to 6

Heat Scale: Mild

MESQUITE-GRILLED CHICKEN
WITH APPLE PISTACHIO CHUTNEY

The chutney is best if made the day before so that the flavors have time to blend. Here we have served it with chicken, but it is also good with fish.

3   green New Mexican chiles, roasted, peeled, stems and seeds removed, chopped

3   tablespoons distilled white vinegar

2   tablespoons orange juice

3   tablespoons brown sugar

3   tart apples, such as Granny Smith or Jonathan, peeled, cored, and chopped

2   tablespoons raisins

3   tablespoons shelled pistachios, coarsely chopped mesquite chips, soaked in water

4   boneless chicken breasts

Combine the chiles, vinegar, orange juice, and brown sugar in a saucepan. Bring to boil, stirring constantly to dissolve the sugar. Add the apples and the raisins and simmer for 30 minutes or until the apples are soft.

Stir in the pistachios and simmer the chutney for 2 more minutes.

Prepare a fire of mesquite wood or charcoal. When the coals have burned down to a medium heat, add the water-soaked mesquite chips. Place the chicken on the grill, skin side down, and grill 10 to 12 minutes. Turn and cook an additional 5 to 6 minutes or until done.

Serve the chicken with the chutney on the side.

Serves: 4
Heat Scale: Medium

EL POLLO AL CARBÓN

The concept of marinating chicken in a spicy fruit juice and then char-broiling originated in Mexico and is becoming quite popular throughout the Southwest. The chicken is served with warm corn tortillas, fresh salsa, and a side of pinto beans. Diners remove the chicken from the bones, place it in the tortilla, top it with salsa, and enjoy.

1 **small onion, chopped**	¼ **teaspoon cinnamon**
2 **cloves garlic, minced**	¼ **teaspoon ground cloves**
2 **tomatillos, husks removed, chopped**	¼ **teaspoon ground Habanero chile**
2 **tablespoons margarine or vegetable oil**	2 **small chickens, cut in half lengthwise**
½ **cup orange juice**	**corn tortillas**
2 **tablespoons lime juice**	**Salsa with Six Names (see recipe, p. 40)**
1 **tablespoon lemon juice**	

Saute the onion, garlic, and tomatillos in the margarine or vegetable oil until soft. Add the remaining ingredients, except the chicken, tortillas, and salsa, and simmer for 10 minutes. Place in a blender and puree to make a sauce.

Marinate the chicken in the sauce for at least 3 hours.

Grill the chicken until done, basting frequently with the sauce. Serve the grilled chicken with the tortillas and salsa.

Note: This recipe requires advance preparation.

Serves: 4

Heat Scale: Hot

CHICKEN AND JICAMA PITA POCKETS

Pita bread makes great pockets for holding a wide variety of fillings, like the one for this recipe. These sandwiches are great for any outing because everything can be prepared the day before—with the exception of the avocado, which should be sliced just before serving so that it doesn't turn brown.

4 green New Mexican chiles, roasted, peeled, stems and seeds removed, chopped	¼ teaspoon ground cumin
	2 cups cooked, diced chicken
¼ cup sour cream or plain yogurt	4 pita bread rounds
	1 cup shredded jicama
¼ cup mayonnaise	2 small tomatoes, diced
1 tablespoon lime juice	shredded lettuce
⅓ cup minced onion	1 avocado, sliced
1 clove garlic, minced	

Combine the first seven ingredients for the dressing and toss with the diced chicken until it's well coated. Marinate the chicken in the refrigerator for at least 4 hours or overnight.

   To serve, cut the pita rounds in half and gently open the pockets with a fork. Combine the chicken, jicama, and tomatoes. Place the lettuce and chicken mixture in the pitas and add the sliced avocado.

Note: This recipe requires advance preparation.

Serves: 4
Heat Scale: Mild

TAMALE PIE WITH CHEESE AND CHICKEN

This recipe is a delicious alternative to traditional tamales. A green salad is all that is needed to complete the meal.

1 4-pound chicken, cut in pieces	1 cup ripe olives, chopped
2 large onions, chopped	1 cup whole-kernel corn
2 cloves garlic, minced	2 cups sour cream
4 green New Mexican chiles, roasted, peeled, stems and seeds removed, chopped	2 cups reserved chicken broth
	1 cup masa harina
	2 eggs, separated
3 jalapeño chiles, stems removed, chopped	2 cups grated Monterey Jack cheese
1 teaspoon ground red New Mexican chile	

Simmer the chicken, half the onion, and the garlic in water to cover until the chicken is done and starts to fall away from the bone. Remove the chicken. Strain the broth and reserve.

Remove the meat from the bones and chop the chicken along with the remaining onion. Combine with the chiles, ground chile, olives, corn, and sour cream. Place the mixture in a casserole dish.

Bring the reserved broth to a boil and gradually add the masa harina, stirring constantly. Reduce the heat and cook until the mixture thickens, about 10 minutes. Remove from the heat and stir in the egg yolks. Whip the egg whites until stiff and fold them into the masa. Spread this batter over the casserole and top with the grated cheese.

Bake for 35 minutes at 375 degrees.

Serves: 6
Heat Scale: Medium

GRAPE-GRILLED QUAIL WITH
GOAT CHEESE ROUNDS

Although many Southwesterners use mesquite for barbecuing and grilling, it is not the only aromatic wood suitable for outdoor cooking. Experiment with pecan, apple, peach, and grape clippings. If you use charcoal for the main fire, be sure to soak the wood for an hour in water before grilling.

2 ancho chiles, stems and seeds removed	2 tablespoons olive oil
⅔ cup olive oil	¼ cup dried corn bread crumbs
¼ cup orange juice	6 6-inch pieces of thick grapevine clippings, soaked in water
2 tablespoons lime juice	
1 clove garlic	Serrano Salsa with Mangoes and Tomatillos (see recipe, p. 41)
12 quail	
6 2-ounce goat cheese rounds	

Simmer the chiles in water for 15 minutes, drain, and puree them in a blender along with the olive oil, the orange and lime juices, and the garlic.

Cut the wing tips off the quail, split the birds down the back, and remove the backbone. With a knife tip, remove the rib bones from each quail, then slice open the thigh to remove the bones and joint, taking care to keep the skin intact. Open up each quail and press the legs together, securing them with toothpicks.

Pour the chile puree over the quail and marinate for an hour.

While the quail are marinating, prepare a medium-hot charcoal fire and preheat the oven to 350 degrees. Brush each goat cheese round with olive oil, coat with corn bread crumbs, and bake for 5 minutes. If you start the baking just when the quail are being grilled, both should be done at the same time.

Add the grapevine clippings to the coals, arrange the quail skin side down on the rack and grill for 2 minutes, taking care not to burn them.

Turn the quail and grill for an additional 2 minutes. If the skin is not yet crisp, turn once more and grill for another minute.

Serve 2 quail on each plate with a goat cheese round. Garnish with the Serrano Salsa.

Serves: 6
Heat Scale: Mild

8

Sizzling Seafood

It may seem surprising to find such a variety of seafood recipes in a Southwestern cookbook—but remember that this region stretches from the Pacific Ocean to the Gulf of Mexico. In between, there are numerous lakes and streams teeming with fish. One of the major differences between Southwestern seafood dishes and those of other areas—such as the Northwest and Northeast Coasts—is the prominent use of chile peppers.

MIXED SEAFOOD CEVICHE WITH THREE KINDS OF CHILES

As is true of so many Central and South American specialties, ceviche (or *seviche* or *serviche*) in its myriad forms has been adopted and transformed by chefs of the Southwest. This version features two different seafoods accompanied by three different chiles.

3   orange Habanero chiles, stems and seeds removed, minced

3   red serrano chiles, stems and seeds removed, minced

3   green jalapeño chiles, stems and seeds removed, minced

½   pound firm fish fillets, cut into 1-inch cubes

½   pound small whole scallops

1   clove garlic, minced

1   medium onion, sliced and separated into rings

2   cups freshly squeezed lime juice

⅓   cup olive oil

3   tablespoons fresh cilantro, minced

Combine all the ingredients in a nonmetallic bowl and marinate in the refrigerator for at least 6 hours, turning occasionally. The fish and scallops should lose their translucency and become opaque. Serve in tall parfait glasses or as a salad over greens and tomatoes.

Note: This recipe requires advance preparation.

Serves: 6 to 8
Heat Scale: Hot

DRUNKEN GULF COAST SHRIMP WITH JALAPEÑOS

Serve this tasty shrimp over white rice accompanied by a green vegetable and a cold beer.

6   red jalapeño chiles, stems
    and seeds removed, minced
1   small onion, chopped fine
1   clove garlic, minced
2   tablespoons olive oil
2   small tomatoes, peeled and
    chopped
⅓   cup tequila
1   teaspoon fresh basil, minced

1   tablespoon fresh cilantro,
    minced
36 large Gulf Coast shrimp,
    peeled and deveined
    flour for dredging
3   tablespoons vegetable oil, or
    more if needed
2   teaspoons cornstarch mixed
    with ¼ cup water

Saute the chiles, onion, and garlic in the oil until soft, then add the tomatoes, tequila, basil, and cilantro and simmer covered for 30 minutes to make a sauce.

Dredge the shrimp in the flour and shake off any excess. In another pan, saute the shrimp in the oil until golden brown. Remove and keep warm.

Stir the cornstarch and water mixture into the sauce and heat until it becomes slightly thickened. Simmer for 5 minutes. Add the shrimp and continue heating for several more minutes or until the shrimp are hot.

Serves: 6
Heat Scale: Hot

BLUE CORN PAN-FRIED TROUT
WITH CHILES DE ÁRBOL

This recipe combines two common ingredients of northern New Mexico, blue corn and fresh trout. Using the blue cornmeal in place of the yellow imparts a nutty flavor to the fish.

2 **whole trout, split open and cleaned**

8 **chiles de árbol, stems and seeds removed, crushed (or substitute other small dried red chiles)**

1 **small onion, thinly sliced and separated into rings**

1 **lemon, sliced in thin rings**

2 **sprigs fresh dill or 1 teaspoon dried dill**

blue cornmeal

vegetable oil for frying

Stuff the fish with the chiles, onion rings, lemon slices, and dill. Roll the fish in the cornmeal and panfry in the oil until browned and done, turning once.

Serves: 2

Heat Scale: Medium

〰〰〰〰〰〰〰

MESQUITE-GRILLED SNAPPER WITH ANCHO SAUCE

Mesquite wood smoke is absorbed by the fish while it grills, imparting a distinctly Southwestern flavor. Care should be taken not to overcook or burn the fish.

THE SAUCE

2 **ancho chiles, stems and seeds removed, chopped**

1 **small onion, chopped**

1 **tablespoon vegetable oil**

2 **small tomatoes, peeled and chopped**

¼ **cup raisins**

2 **cups chicken broth**

THE FISH

mesquite wood, or mesquite chips soaked in water

4 **snapper fillets**

olive oil

Saute the chiles and onion in the vegetable oil until soft. Add the tomatoes, raisins, and broth and simmer for an additional 10 minutes.

Place the mixture in a blender and puree until smooth. Keep the sauce warm.

Prepare a fire of mesquite wood or add mesquite chips to a charcoal fire. When the coals have burned down to a medium heat, rub the fillets with olive oil and grill for 4 or 5 minutes per side, turning once. Turning more often could cause the fillets to fall apart.

Place the fish on individual plates, pour the sauce over the fish, and serve.

Serves: 4
Heat Scale: Mild

CAMARONES AL MOJO DE AJO

This garlic shrimp dish hails from Guerrero, Mexico, but is commonly served in Mexican seafood restaurants in the Southwest. The shrimp are messy to peel and eat, but they are delicious.

1 tablespoon ground red New Mexican chile	1 teaspoon vinegar
10 cloves garlic, minced salt and freshly ground black pepper to taste	24 large shrimp, unpeeled 2 tablespoons olive oil 4 tablespoons butter 2 tablespoons lime juice

Crush together the ground chile, garlic, salt, pepper, and vinegar in a *molcajete* or mortar and marinate the shrimp in the mixture for 1 hour.

Heat the oil and butter in a skillet, add the garlic marinade, and saute for 3 minutes. Add the shrimp and saute another 3 minutes, turning often. Sprinkle the shrimp with lime juice and serve.

Serves: 4
Heat Scale: Medium

GORDITAS CON LANGOSTOS

These "little fat ones" are served along the Texas-Mexico border where they are traditionally filled with beans or shredded meat. This recipe features seafood—either lobster or crab—stuffed in a masa pastry.

THE GORDITAS

1 cup masa harina	½ teaspoon salt
2 cups flour	1⅓ cups warm water
1½ teaspoons baking powder	vegetable oil for frying

Combine the masa harina, flour, baking powder, and salt. Add the water slowly and knead to form a stiff dough. Cover the dough with plastic wrap and allow to sit for 15 minutes.

Divide the dough into 6 portions and form into balls. Roll out each ball to a circle about ¼ inch thick. Fry the gorditas in 350-degree oil until puffed and browned. Remove and drain. They will be hollow inside.

THE FILLING

3 green New Mexican chiles, roasted, peeled, stems and seeds removed, chopped	2 tomatoes, peeled and chopped
¼ cup chopped bell pepper	½ pound lobster meat or lump crabmeat
1 small onion, chopped	
2 tablespoons butter or margarine	

Saute the chiles, bell pepper, and onion in the butter. Add the tomatoes and simmer for an additional 10 minutes. Stir in the lobster meat and cook until heated.

To serve, cut off the end of a gordita, stuff with the lobster mixture, and keep warm in the oven. These gorditas are eaten like sandwiches.

Serves: 6
Heat Scale: Medium

SEAFOOD FLAUTAS

Here's one of those quick and tasty supper dishes that can just as easily be an appetizer. For heartier flautas, use tuna or salmon.

1 **pound firm white fish, such as snapper or halibut**	1 **small tomato, peeled and seeded, chopped**
2 **tablespoons olive oil**	1 **teaspoon dried oregano**
1 **onion, chopped**	¼ **teaspoon ground cinnamon**
2 **cloves garlic, minced**	12 **corn tortillas**
3 **jalapeños *en escabeche*, stems removed, chopped**	1 **cup grated asadero cheese vegetable oil for frying**

Saute the fish in the oil until done. Remove and flake the fish, using two forks.

Add the onion and garlic to the pan and saute until soft. Add the next 4 ingredients and simmer until the liquid has evaporated. Stir the fish into the sauce.

To assemble, heat the tortillas briefly on a hot griddle to soften. Put 2 tablespoons of the fish mixture on a tortilla, add some cheese, and roll up tightly. Secure the flauta with a toothpick to hold it together.

Heat 2 inches of oil in a skillet. Fry the flautas until golden brown. Remove and drain.

Yield: 12
Heat Scale: Mild

GRILLED TOMATILLO SHRIMP

The heat of this spicy kebab is controlled by the number of jalapeño strips used. Milder fresh chiles can also be substituted to tame this dish.

2 tomatillos	2 tablespoons chopped fresh cilantro
2 tablespoons minced onion	
1 clove garlic, minced	1 pound shelled shrimp, tails left on
1 tablespoon olive oil	
¼ cup lime juice, fresh preferred	4–6 jalapeños, stems and seeds removed, cut in strips
freshly ground black pepper	

Place the tomatillos on a hot skillet and roast for several minutes until blackened on all sides.

In another pan, saute the onion and garlic in the oil until soft.

Place the tomatillos, onion mixture, lime juice, and black pepper in a blender and puree until smooth. Stir in the cilantro.

Marinate the shrimp in the mixture for an hour. Remove and thread on skewers along with the chile strips. Place the marinade in a pan and heat.

Grill the kebabs until just done (a few minutes on each side) and serve with the sauce on the side.

Serves: 4
Heat Scale: Hot

〰〰〰〰〰〰〰〰

TEXAS CRAB CAKES WITH JALAPEÑO CREAM

Crab is a favorite around the Texas Gulf Coast where it is plentiful and available almost year-round. This recipe combines that favorite with another, jalapeños, to create a spicy entree.

THE FISH

2 jalapeño chiles, stems and seeds removed, finely chopped
½ cup finely chopped onion
¼ cup finely chopped celery
¼ cup finely chopped bell pepper
1 tablespoon olive oil
1 pound crabmeat
2 cups dry bread crumbs

1 tablespoon chopped parsley
1 tablespoon lemon juice
2 teaspoons Worcestershire sauce
½ teaspoon ground cayenne
2 eggs
½ cup milk
flour
vegetable oil

Saute the jalapeños, onion, celery, and bell pepper in the olive oil.

Combine the jalapeño mixture with the crab, one cup of the bread crumbs, parsley, lemon juice, Worcestershire sauce, and cayenne. Beat 1 of the eggs and add to the crab mixture. Refrigerate for 1 hour. Shape the crab mixture into 6 patties, or cakes.

Beat the remaining egg with milk. Dip each cake in the flour, then in the egg mixture, and finally in the remaining bread crumbs. Refrigerate for an additional hour.

Heat the vegetable oil to 350 degrees. Fry each cake on both sides until browned. Top with the jalapeño cream and serve.

Serves: 4 to 6
Heat Scale: Medium

THE SAUCE

2 tablespoons minced onion
1 clove garlic, minced
2 tablespoons butter or margarine
3 jalapeño chiles, stems and seeds removed, chopped

2 tablespoons sour cream
2 cups heavy cream or half-and-half

Saute the onion and garlic in the butter. Add the chiles and continue to saute for an additional 2 minutes. Stir in the sour cream and cream, bring to a boil, reduce the heat, and simmer until the sauce has thickened.

Yield: 2 cups
Heat Scale: Medium

TAMALES WITH SHRIMP

Putting shrimp inside tamales may sound strange but it's very popular along the west coast of Mexico and up into California. For a different-tasting tamale, try substituting other seafood for the shrimp.

2	ancho chiles, stems and seeds removed	2	pounds shrimp, shelled and deveined
2	dried red New Mexican chiles, stems and seeds removed		corn husks
1	large onion, chopped	4	cups masa harina
2	cloves garlic, minced	1	teaspoon salt
2	tablespoons vegetable oil	2½–3	cups broth or water
3	small tomatoes, peeled and finely chopped	⅔	cup lard or shortening
1	teaspoon ground cumin	1	cup grated Monterey Jack cheese

Cover the chiles with hot water and simmer them for 15 minutes until softened. Place the chiles, along with a little of the water in which they soaked, into a blender and puree until smooth.

Saute the onion and garlic in the oil until softened. Add the chiles, tomatoes, and cumin. Bring to a boil, reduce the heat, and simmer until the sauce is reduced and thickened.

Add the shrimp and simmer for an additional 10 minutes. Cool the mixture before assembling the tamales.

Soak the corn husks in water to soften.

Mix together the masa harina and salt. Slowly add the broth, stirring with a fork until the mixture holds together. Whip the lard or shortening until fluffy. Add the masa harina to the shortening and continue to beat. Drop a teaspoonful of dough into a glass of cold water. If the dough floats, it is ready. If it sinks, continue to beat it until it floats.

To assemble, select corn husks that measure about 5 by 8 inches or overlap smaller ones together. Place 2 tablespoons of masa in the center of the husk and pat or spread the dough evenly into a 2-by-3–inch rectangle. Place 2 to 3 shrimp plus some of the sauce down the center and top with some cheese. Fold the husk around the masa and filling, being careful not to squeeze the tamale.

There are two basic ways of securing the corn husks. The first is to use two strips of husk to firmly tie each end of the tamale. This method works well with smaller husks.

The second method is to fold the tapered end over the filled husk and then fold the remaining end over it. Tie the tamale around the middle with a strip of husk to keep the ends folded down.

Place a rack in the bottom of a steamer or large pot. Make sure that the rack is high enough to keep the tamales above the water. Place the tamales on the rack, folded side down; if the pot is large enough, stand them up. Do not pack them tightly because they need to expand as they cook. Cover with additional husks or a towel to absorb the moisture. Bring the water to a boil, reduce to a gentle boil, and steam for an hour for each dozen tamales or until done. To test for doneness, open one end of a husk; if the masa pulls away from the wrapper, it is done.

Yield: 24
Heat Scale: Medium

~~~~~~~~~~~~~~~~

CRAB-STUFFED CHAYOTE AU GRATIN

Members of the gourd family, chayotes were first cultivated by both the Aztecs and the Mayas. Chayotes are beginning to show up in grocery stores in the Southwest, and they're also popular in Louisiana, where they're called "mirlitons."

4 chayotes
2 tablespoons chopped green onion
2 tablespoons chopped celery
2 cloves garlic, minced
3 jalapeño chiles, stems and seeds removed, chopped
4 tablespoons butter or margarine
¼ teaspoon dill
2 tablespoons flour
1 cup cream or half-and-half
½ cup white wine
1 pound cooked crabmeat
½ cup grated Monterey Jack cheese

Cut the chayotes in half and remove the seeds. Boil until tender, about 20 to 25 minutes. Scoop out the pulp (taking care not to break the skin) to reserve for stuffing.

Saute the onion, celery, garlic, and jalapeños in half the butter until soft. Stir in the dill.

Melt the remaining butter and stir in the flour. Saute the roux for several minutes, being careful not to let it brown. Stir in the cream and wine and simmer until thickened.

Combine the sauce, jalapeño mixture, chayote pulp, and crab. Spoon into the chayote shells and top with the cheese.

Bake for 15 minutes at 350 degrees.

Serves: 4
Heat Scale: Mild

9

Los Huevos y los Quesos y los Otros

The eggs, the cheeses, and the others are combination dishes often served at breakfast, although they can be devoured at any time. They range from stuffed chiles to casseroles to quiches to pastas.

HUEVOS RANCHEROS OF
THE GREAT SOUTHWEST

Although the recipe may vary from place to place, the bottom line with ranch-style eggs is that they are delicious for a hearty breakfast or a brunch served with refried beans and hash brown potatoes.

TEX-MEX VERSION

4 jalapeño chiles, stems and seeds removed, chopped

1 small onion, chopped

2 tablespoons vegetable oil

2 medium tomatoes, chopped

vegetable oil for frying

4 corn tortillas

8 eggs

½ cup grated Monterey Jack cheese for garnish

Saute the jalapeños and onion in the oil until soft. Add the tomatoes and cook down to a thick sauce.

Heat 2 inches of oil in a pan. Fry each tortilla in the oil for only a few seconds per side until soft. Remove and drain on paper towels.

Fry each egg in the oil to desired consistency.

To serve, place the sauce on each tortilla and gently slip the eggs on top of the sauce. Garnish with the grated cheese.

Serves: 4

Heat Scale: Medium

NEW MEXICAN VERSION

2 cups Classic Red or Green Chile Sauce (see recipes, pp. 46 and 47)

8 eggs

vegetable oil for frying

4 corn tortillas

1 medium tomato, chopped, for garnish

Heat the chile sauce in a frying pan.

Crack the eggs in the sauce, cover with a lid, and poach to desired consistency.

Heat 2 inches of oil in a pan. Fry each tortilla in the oil for only a few seconds per side until soft. Remove and drain on paper towels.

To serve, slip the eggs with the sauce onto the tortillas and garnish with the tomatoes.

Variation: Sprinkle with grated cheddar cheese.

Serves: 4

Heat Scale: Medium

SOUTHERN CALIFORNIA VERSION

¼ cup chopped onion

1 clove garlic, chopped

1 tablespoon vegetable oil

1 cup chopped tomatoes

3 green New Mexican chiles, roasted, peeled, stems and seeds removed, chopped

vegetable oil for frying

4 corn tortillas

8 eggs

1 cup refried beans

½ cup grated cheddar cheese for garnish

chopped black olives for garnish

sour cream for garnish

Saute the onions and garlic in the oil. Add the tomatoes and chiles and simmer until the sauce has thickened.

Heat 2 inches of oil in a pan. Fry each tortilla in the oil for only a few seconds per side until soft. Remove and drain on paper towels.

Fry the eggs in the oil, sunny-side up, to desired consistency.

To assemble, spread the beans on each tortilla, place some sauce on each, and top with the eggs. Garnish with the grated cheese, chopped olives, a dollop of sour cream, and serve.

Serves: 4

Heat Scale: Mild

MIGAS

This simple but delicious egg dish hails from Texas and is particularly loved in Austin. It can be made with any fresh or cooked salsa. In Texas it would likely be made with the Salsa with Six Names (p. 40) or Tomatillo Sauce with Cilantro (p. 45).

	vegetable oil	½	cup salsa or chile sauce (see Chapter 4)
2	corn tortillas, cut into eighths	4	tablespoons grated Monterey Jack cheese
2	eggs, beaten		

Heat 2 inches of oil in a pan and fry the tortilla pieces until crisp. Remove the tortillas and drain off all but 2 teaspoons of the oil.

Place the tortilla pieces back in the pan. Add the eggs, stir, and cook over low heat until the eggs are set. Add the salsa or sauce and stir until heated throughout.

Sprinkle the cheese on top and serve.

Serves: 1
Heat Scale: Varies

QUICHE MACHO-STYLE

''Real'' men will certainly eat this hot quiche! Serve with a crisp garden salad, minted fresh fruit, and a glass of chilled white wine. Okay, okay, make that a chilled Mexican beer.

1   10-inch pastry shell
6   green New Mexican chiles, roasted, peeled, stems and seeds removed, chopped
1   cup grated Swiss cheese
¼   cup sliced black olives
2   eggs
2   egg yolks

1½ cups heavy cream or milk, scalded and cooled
1   cup cooked whole-kernel corn
2   tablespoons finely chopped green onions
½   teaspoon salt

Line the bottom of the pastry shell with the chopped green chiles. Top with the cheese and olives.

Combine the eggs and egg yolks with the cream and beat well. Stir in the corn, green onions, and salt. Pour this mixture into the pastry shell.

Bake at 350 degrees for 30 to 40 minutes or until the custard has set.

Serves: 4 to 6
Heat Scale: Medium

~~~~~~~~~~~~~~~~

CHIPOTLE *CHILAQUILES*

Ah, the wonderful, smoky-hot flavor of the chipotle comes through in this breakfast classic. It can be baked or microwaved—either way, it takes only a few minutes to prepare.

2   tomatoes, chopped
4   chipotle peppers in *adobo,* chopped
2   cloves garlic, chopped
½   onion, chopped
½   cup chicken stock
    vegetable oil

6   corn tortillas, cut into eighths
4   eggs, beaten
1   cup grated Monterey Jack or cheddar cheese
    chopped cilantro for garnish

Combine the tomatoes, chipotles, garlic, onion, and stock in a blender and puree to make a sauce. Bring the sauce to a boil, reduce the heat, and simmer for 15 minutes or until the sauce is thickened.

Heat 2 inches of oil in a pan. Fry each tortilla in the oil for only a few seconds per side until soft. Remove and drain on paper towels.

Combine the sauce and eggs.

To assemble the casserole, line the bottom of a small casserole dish with tortilla wedges, then add ⅓ of the sauce mixture, and top with ⅓ of the cheese. Repeat twice more.

Bake the casserole in a 300-degree oven for 15 minutes or microwave on high for about 5 minutes.

Garnish with the cilantro and serve.

Serves: 2 to 4
Heat Scale: Medium

∿∿∿∿∿∿∿∿∿∿∿∿

BLUE CORN PIÑON PANCAKES WITH ORANGE-SPICED HONEY

Here's one of our favorite breakfast dishes. The blue corn makes these pancakes a refreshing change from the ordinary.

THE HONEY

½ cup honey
¼ cup orange juice
1 teaspoon grated orange peel

pinch of dried crushed Habanero chile (or other hot chile)

Place the honey in a saucepan and heat. Stir in the remaining ingredients and keep warm.

Yield: ¾ cup
Heat Scale: Hot

THE PANCAKES

1 cup blue corn flour	1 cup buttermilk
½ cup all-purpose flour	3 tablespoons melted butter or margarine
3 tablespoons sugar	
1¾ teaspoons double-acting baking powder	3 tablespoons roasted piñon nuts
1 large egg, beaten	

Sift together all the dry ingredients. Combine the liquid ingredients and beat well.

Quickly mix the liquids into the dry ingredients, being careful not to overbeat the mixture—lumps are okay.

Cook the pancakes on a hot griddle, turning only once, until browned and done.

Serve with the warm honey.

Yield: 1 dozen 4-inch pancakes
Heat Scale: Medium

ROASTED POBLANO CHILES WITH
SPICED GOAT CHEESE

Usually milder than New Mexican chiles, poblanos impart a distinctive taste to these rellenos. The filling is a combination of traditional Mexican and New Southwest ingredients.

2 teaspoons ground red New Mexican chile	flour for dredging
½ cup goat cheese	4 eggs, separated
½ cup ricotta cheese	4 tablespoons flour
1 cup walnuts, chopped fine	2 teaspoons baking powder
½ cup raisins	1 tablespoon water
¼ teaspoon ground cinnamon	¼ teaspoon salt
¼ teaspoon ground cloves	vegetable oil for frying
4 large poblano chiles, roasted and peeled, stems left on	

Combine the first 7 ingredients to make the filling. Make a slit in the side of each pepper and stuff with the filling. Roll each chile in the flour and shake off the excess.

Beat the egg whites until stiff. Combine the egg yolks and the remaining ingredients (except the oil) and gently fold into the egg whites to make a batter.

Carefully dip the chiles into the batter and coat well. Heat 2 to 3 inches of oil in a pan to 350 degrees. Add the chiles and fry until lightly browned, turning once. Remove and drain on paper towels.

Serves: 4
Heat Scale: Mild

FETTUCINE PASTA WITH GREEN CHILE PESTO

This Southwestern adaptation of an Italian specialty uses green chile and spinach in place of the traditional basil in the pesto.

THE PESTO

6 green New Mexican chiles, roasted, peeled, stems and seeds removed, chopped
½ cup olive oil
2 cups fresh spinach, chopped
½ cup chopped fresh cilantro or parsley

2 cloves garlic
1 tablespoon chopped fresh basil or 2 teaspoons dried
2 tablespoons piñon nuts
   salt and pepper to taste

Puree all the ingredients to make a smooth sauce. Thin with water to process if necessary.

Yield: 1 to 1½ cups
Heat Scale: Medium

THE PASTA

3 quarts of water
   salt
½ pound fettuccine

olive oil
grated Romano cheese

Bring the water to a boil and add the salt and fettuccine. Cook uncovered until tender but still firm—*al dente,* as the Italians say. Drain and toss with a few drops of olive oil so the pasta does not stick together.

To serve, toss the fettuccine with the pesto until well coated. Garnish with the cheese and additional piñon nuts if desired.

Serves: 4 to 6
Heat Scale: Medium

SOUTHWESTERN LASAGNA

If you love to make your own pasta, try substituting blue corn flour for wheat flour when making lasagna noodles. The color and flavor are definitely not Italian.

¾ **pound homemade chorizo sausage (see recipe, p. 77) or commercial chorizo, removed from the casing**
1 **large onion, chopped**
3 **cloves garlic, chopped**
1 **tablespoon vegetable oil**
2 **tablespoons ground red New Mexican chile**
1 **pound tomatoes, peeled, seeds removed**
¼ **cup tomato paste**
1 **tablespoon chopped fresh cilantro**

½ **teaspoon sugar**
 salt and pepper to taste
12–14 **strips of lasagna noodles**
4 **quarts water**
2 **cups ricotta cheese**
1 **egg, lightly beaten**
6 **green New Mexican chiles, roasted, peeled, stems and seeds removed, cut in strips**
½ **pound mozzarella cheese, thinly sliced**

Saute the sausage, onion, and garlic in the oil until soft. Pour off any excess oil.

Add the ground chile, tomatoes, tomato paste, cilantro, sugar, and salt and pepper to taste. Bring to a boil, reduce the heat, and simmer for 30 to 45 minutes or until thick.

Cook the lasagna noodles in 4 quarts of boiling salted water until just done. Drain.

Combine the ricotta cheese and the egg.

To assemble, place a layer of noodles in a greased pan. Top with a layer of the cheese mixture, sauce, green chile strips, and mozzarella. Repeat the procedure, ending with the mozzarella.

Bake in a 350-degree oven for 30 minutes or until thoroughly heated. Allow to stand for 10 minutes before cutting.

Serves: 6 to 8
Heat Scale: Medium

PECOS VALLEY PASTA PIE

Substitute or add ingredients, such as chorizo and green New Mexican chile, to create a variety of different pies.

THE FILLING

½ pound ground beef

1 medium onion, chopped fine

8 jalapeño chiles, stems and seeds removed, chopped fine

2 tablespoons commercial chili powder

1 small bell pepper, chopped fine

1 cup canned tomatoes, chopped

1 cup cooked pinto beans

1 pound macaroni

4 quarts water

1 egg, beaten

Saute the beef, onion, jalapeños, chili powder, and bell pepper until the meat is no longer pink. Add the tomatoes and pinto beans and simmer for 10 minutes.

Cook the macaroni in 4 quarts of boiling salted water until almost done—the macaroni should be fairly firm. Drain and reserve the water.

Combine the macaroni and meat mixture.

Prepare the cheese sauce and stir it into the macaroni mixture.

Prepare the pastry dough and divide it into two balls, one a little larger than the other. Roll out the dough. Line a greased 10-inch cake pan with a removable bottom with the larger amount of dough. Pour the macaroni mixture into the pan. Place the remaining dough on top and pinch together to seal. Brush with the egg and prick with a fork.

Bake in a 375-degree oven for 40 to 50 minutes or until golden brown. Allow the pie to sit for 10 minutes before removing from the pan.

Serves: 6 to 8
Heat Scale: Mild

THE SAUCE

6 tablespoons butter or margarine	¼ teaspoon dry mustard
6 tablespoons flour	3 cups milk
¼ teaspoon cayenne powder	1 cup grated cheddar cheese

Melt the butter and stir in the flour. Simmer for 2 to 3 minutes, making sure that the flour does not brown. Stir in the cayenne and mustard.

Add the milk all at once and stir until smooth. Simmer for 2 minutes. Add the cheese and continue to cook for 3 to 4 minutes, stirring constantly, or until thickened.

Yield: 2 to 2½ cups

Heat Scale: Mild

THE PASTRY

⅓ cup lard or shortening	1 egg
⅓ cup butter or margarine	½ teaspoon salt
2 cups flour	3–4 tablespoons cold water

Cut the shortening and butter into the flour until the mixture is crumbly. Add the egg, salt, and water and mix until the dough is completely moistened.

Divide into two unequal balls. Wrap in wax paper and refrigerate for 1 hour before rolling out.

FIERY FRITTATA

This hearty omelet can be served for brunch or lunch as well as breakfast. Other fresh chiles and even vegetables can be added to give the dish a different taste.

2 large potatoes, cooked and diced

½ cup chopped onion

¼ cup olive oil

6 green New Mexican chiles, roasted, peeled, stems and seeds removed, cut in wide strips

¼ cup chopped olives

1 cup shredded Monterey Jack cheese

8 eggs, beaten

¼ cup milk

In a skillet, saute the potatoes and onion in the oil until the potatoes are browned. Top the potato mixture with the chiles, olives, and grated cheese.

Combine the eggs and milk. Pour the egg mixture over the potato mixture and stir gently. Reduce the heat to low, cover, and cook until the eggs are almost set.

Place the skillet uncovered under the broiler to brown slightly. Cut into wedges and serve.

Serves: 8
Heat Scale: Mild

10

A Harvest of Wholesome Heat

C hile peppers are high in vitamins A and C, low in sodium, high in fiber, and of course have no cholesterol. When combined with other vegetables, as in these recipes, they create very healthy hot dishes.

CALABACITAS CON CHILES VERDES

Squash and corn are familiar accompaniments throughout the Southwest. This recipe is particularly good with traditional entrees such as enchiladas, tamales, and burritos.

1 cup chopped onion	2 medium zucchini, sliced
2 cloves garlic, minced	1 cup whole-kernel corn
1 tablespoon bacon drippings or vegetable oil	⅓ cup cream or half-and-half
4 green New Mexican chiles, roasted, peeled, stems and seeds removed, chopped	

Saute the onion and garlic in the drippings until soft.

Add the chiles, zucchini, and corn. Simmer for 15 or 20 minutes or until the squash is almost done.

Add the cream, increase the heat until the cream starts to boil, and cook until the vegetables are done and the sauce is thick.

Serves: 6
Heat Scale: Medium

〜〜〜〜〜〜〜〜〜〜

PAPAS CON CHILE COLORADO

Although the word *colorado* here refers to the red color of the chile rather than the state of the same name, this dish is commonly prepared there—and all over the Southwest. Serve these red chile potatoes in place of hash browns for a terrific Southwestern breakfast.

½ cup chopped onion
1 clove garlic, minced
2 tablespoons butter or margarine
2 tablespoons crushed red New Mexican chile, including the seeds

2 large potatoes, peeled and diced
1 tablespoon grated Parmesan cheese

Saute the onion and garlic in the butter until soft, then add the chile. Toss the potatoes in the mixture.

Place the potatoes in a shallow pan with a little water and bake in a 350-degree oven until the potatoes are done, about 45 minutes.

Sprinkle the cheese over the top of the potatoes and serve.

Serves: 4
Heat Scale: Medium

~~~~~~~~~~~~~~~~

SWEET AND HOT GLAZED CARROTS

The sweet spiciness of the glaze complements the heat of the chile to produce a vegetable treat that goes great with any roasted, grilled, or baked meats.

1 pound carrots, cut in julienne
4 teaspoons ground red New Mexican chile

2 tablespoons butter
1 tablespoon honey
½ teaspoon cinnamon

Steam the carrots until tender but still slightly crisp. Combine the remaining ingredients and simmer for 10 minutes. Toss the carrots in the glaze until coated and serve.

Serves: 6
Heat Scale: Medium

CORN AND JALAPEÑO CUSTARD

This unusual creation can be served either as a vegetarian entree or as a vegetable second course. Double the amount of jalapeños for a more daring dish.

2	tablespoons jalapeño chiles, stems and seeds removed, chopped	¼	cup whole milk
½	cup creamed corn	¼	cup minced onion
½	cup cooked rice	¼	cup chopped black olives
½	cup grated cheddar cheese	1	egg, beaten
¼	cup yellow cornmeal	½	teaspoon ground cumin
		½	teaspoon salt
		⅛	teaspoon baking powder

Combine all the ingredients and place in a greased 8-by-8–inch baking dish. Bake at 350 degrees for 30 minutes or until set and lightly browned.

Serves: 4 to 6
Heat Scale: Mild

〜〜〜〜〜〜〜〜〜〜

MARINATED CHIPOTLE ZUCCHINI

One of the chiles of choice when preparing Southwestern food, the chipotle imparts a wonderful smoky-hot flavor to the squash.

3–4	tablespoons olive oil	1	tablespoon wine vinegar
1	medium onion, cut in ¼-inch slices	1	canned chipotle in *adobo,* chopped
4	small zucchini, cut in half lengthwise		chopped fresh cilantro or parsley

Heat the oil and saute the onion until soft. Place the zucchini halves, cut sides down, on top of the onion. Reduce the heat, cover the pan, and cook for 20 minutes or until tender. Remove the vegetables and keep warm.

Stir in the vinegar and chipotle. Add more oil if necessary. Simmer the marinade for several minutes to blend the flavors.

Place the zucchini on a plate and top with the onions. Pour the marinade over the top and allow to marinate for 15 to 20 minutes.

Top with the chopped cilantro and serve either warm or at room temperature.

Serves: 8
Heat Scale: Medium

〰〰〰〰〰〰〰〰〰〰

CHILE-CHEESE BROCCOLI CASSEROLE

Although broccoli—a close relative of cabbage and cauliflower—was grown in Williamsburg, Virginia, as early as 1775, it disappeared from American recipes until the mid-twentieth century. This combination of the vegetable with chile peppers and cheese is a good example of the adoption of ''foreign'' elements into Southwestern cuisines.

4   green New Mexican chiles, roasted, peeled, stems and seeds removed, chopped

1½   pounds fresh broccoli, steamed but firm, drained, and chopped

½   pound mushrooms, sliced and sauteed briefly in butter

4   tablespoons butter or margarine

4   tablespoons flour

2   cups milk

2   tablespoons grated onion

1¾   cup grated sharp cheddar cheese

½   teaspoon each salt, cayenne powder, freshly ground black pepper

Mix the chiles, broccoli, and mushrooms together and place in a casserole dish.

Melt the butter in a small saucepan, add the flour, and simmer for 2 minutes. Reduce the heat, add the milk, and stir constantly until the mixture thickens. Add the onion, cheese, and spices and cook for 2 minutes, stirring constantly.

Pour the cheese sauce over the vegetables, cover, and bake at 325 degrees for 30 minutes.

Serves: 6
Heat Scale: Medium

CHILES RELLENOS

Chiles rellenos literally means "stuffed chiles," and in Mexico many different chiles are used, including poblanos, jalapeños, rocotos, and even fresh pasillas. Here in the Southwest, we prefer New Mexican green chiles. Whichever chile you use, the preparation and fillings are the same.

1 medium onion, chopped	6 green New Mexican chiles, roasted and peeled, stems left on
2 cloves garlic, minced	
2 tablespoons butter or margarine	flour for dredging
2½ cups cooked whole-kernel corn	3 eggs, separated
	1 tablespoon water
1 teaspoon dried oregano	3 tablespoons flour
⅓ cup sour cream	¼ teaspoon salt
6 ounces cheddar cheese, cubed	vegetable oil

Saute the onion and garlic in the butter until soft. Add the corn and oregano and cook for an additional 5 minutes. Remove from the heat and stir in the sour cream and cheese.

Make a slit in the side of each chile and stuff with the corn mixture. Dredge the chiles in the flour and shake off any excess.

Beat the egg whites until they form stiff peaks. Beat the yolks with the water, the three tablespoons of flour, and the salt. Fold the yolks into the whites.

Dip the chiles in the egg batter and fry in 1 to 2 inches of oil until they are golden brown. You can serve the rellenos with a red or green chile sauce.

Serves: 6
Heat Scale: Mild

ORANGE-GLAZED FIERY GREEN BEANS

These sweet and spicy green beans are an excellent accompaniment for roast pork, beef, or lamb as well as poultry or fish dishes.

4 serrano chiles, stems removed, cut in thin strips

1 pound french cut green beans

2 tablespoons orange juice

2 teaspoons orange zest or grated orange peel

¼ cup butter or margarine

¼ cup light brown sugar

Combine the chiles, green beans, orange juice, and orange zest. Allow to marinate for an hour.

Melt the butter, add the sugar, and heat until dissolved.

Add the green bean mixture and simmer until the beans are glazed and cooked.

Serves: 4
Heat Scale: Medium

SPICY GRILLED ONIONS

These onions go well with a variety of foods, such as steaks, fajitas, and hamburgers. Marinate the onions overnight and throw them on the grill while cooking the entree.

1 tablespoon ground red New Mexican chile
1 cup olive oil
3 cloves garlic, minced

18–24 large green onions, including 3 to 4 inches of the green

Combine all the ingredients and marinate the onions for at least 4 hours. Grill over hot coals until all sides are browned.

Note: This recipe requires advance preparation.

Serves: 6
Heat Scale: Mild

∿∿∿∿∿∿∿∿

SOUTHWEST SUMMER VEGETABLES

This recipe combines a variety of summer vegetables—use whatever you have available. Serve in a flour tortilla for an unusual meatless burrito.

¼ cup olive oil
2 tablespoons red wine vinegar
1 tablespoon crushed red New Mexican chile, including the seeds
1 tablespoon chopped fresh cilantro
¼ teaspoon crushed cumin seeds

4 ears of corn, cut into 2-inch lengths
1 bell pepper, stem and seeds removed, cut in wedges
2 large onions, cut into 1½-inch pieces
2 zucchinis, cut in 1-inch rounds
cherry tomatoes

Combine the oil, vinegar, chile, cilantro, and cumin. Simmer for several minutes to blend the flavors.

Thread the vegetables on skewers and grill for 7 to 10 minutes or until done, basting frequently with the sauce.

Variation: Thread 2-inch slices of commercial chorizo sausage (in casing) along with the vegetables.

Serves: 4 to 6

Heat Scale: Mild

BLUE CORN VEGETABLE TAMALES

Blue corn, native to the Southwest, gives these tamales a distinctive, nutty taste. Make them smaller than an entree tamale and serve as a side dish in place of a vegetable.

6 green New Mexico chiles, roasted, peeled, stems and seeds removed, chopped	2 cups coarse blue cornmeal
	1 teaspoon salt
2 cups whole-kernel corn	2 cups chicken broth
¾ cup shredded cheddar cheese corn husks	⅓ cup lard or shortening

Combine the chiles, corn, and cheese together for the filling.

Soak the corn husks in water to soften.

Mix together the blue cornmeal and salt. Slowly add the broth, stirring with a fork until the mixture holds together. Whip the lard or shortening until fluffy. Add the cornmeal mixture to the shortening and continue to beat. Drop a teaspoonful of dough into a glass of cold water. If the dough floats, it is ready. If it sinks, continue to beat it until it floats.

To assemble, select corn husks that measure about 5 by 8 inches or overlap smaller ones together. Place 2 tablespoons of dough in the center of the husk and pat or spread it evenly into a 2-by-3-inch rectangle. Place

2 to 3 tablespoons of the filling down the center and top with some cheese. Fold the husk around the dough and filling, being careful not to squeeze the tamale.

There are two basic ways of securing the corn husks. The first is to use two strips of husk to firmly tie each end of the tamale. This method works well with smaller corn husks.

The second method is to fold the tapered end over the filled husk and then fold the remaining end over it. Tie the tamale around the middle with a strip of husk to keep the ends folded down.

Place a rack in the bottom of a steamer or large pot. Make sure that the rack is high enough to keep the tamales above the water. Place the tamales on the rack, folded side down; if the pot is large enough, stand them up. Do not pack them tightly because they need to expand as they cook. Cover with additional husks or a towel to absorb the moisture. Bring the water to a boil, reduce to a gentle boil, and steam for an hour for each dozen tamales or until done. To test for doneness, open one end of a husk; if the dough pulls away from the wrapper, it is done.

Yield: 24

Heat Scale: Mild

TEXAS JALAPEÑO ONION RINGS

These fiery onion rings go with any barbecue or can take the place of french fries to spice up a hamburger plate.

5 jalapeño chiles, stems and seeds removed, chopped	1 egg, beaten vegetable oil for frying
12 ounces beer, at room temperature	3 large onions, sliced in rings ¼ inch thick, separated
1⅓ cups flour	

Place the chiles in a blender with a little of the beer and puree. Combine the remaining beer with the flour and egg to form a batter.

Pour about 1 to 1½ inches of oil in a skillet and heat to 350 degrees.

Dip the onion rings in the batter and drain the excess. Fry in the oil until golden brown. Remove and drain.

Serves: 4 to 6
Heat Scale: Medium

~~~~~~~~~~~~~~~~

PUEBLO CHILE FRITTERS

The Pueblo Indians were making chile fritters when the Spanish arrived. We have made some changes to the traditional recipe for a more contemporary taste.

⅓ cup water
⅓ cup all-purpose white flour
1 egg, slightly beaten
½ teaspoon baking powder
4 green New Mexican chiles, roasted, peeled, stems and seeds removed, chopped

¼ cup whole-kernel corn
2 tablespoons chopped onion
vegetable oil for frying

Slowly add the water to the flour, stirring constantly, to make a thin sauce. Add the remaining ingredients except the oil and mix well.

Drop the batter by tablespoons into 350-degree oil and fry until golden brown. Remove and drain.

Yield: 12 fritters
Heat Scale: Medium

The Pods,
the Grains,
and the Flours

O r as we sometimes say, the beans, the rice, and the breads. All are staple foods spiced up with Southwestern touches— and believe it or not, some do *not* contain chile peppers!

FRIJOLES BORRACHOS

Not only do these ''drunken'' beans contain fine Mexican beer, they are usually consumed with the same.

2   cups pinto beans, sorted and rinsed clean

¼   cup chopped jalapeño chiles, stems removed

12   ounces dark Mexican beer, such as Negra Modelo

1   small onion, chopped

1   large tomato, peeled and chopped

1   teaspoon Worcestershire sauce

Cover the beans with water, soak overnight, then drain.

Cover the beans with fresh water, bring to a boil, reduce the heat, and simmer until the beans are done, about 2 to 2½ hours. Remove and drain, reserving 1 to 2 cups of the bean water.

Combine the remaining ingredients, the beans, and the reserved bean liquid. Simmer for 30 minutes to blend the flavors or until the liquid has been reduced to the desired amount.

Serving Suggestions: Serve as an accompaniment to any barbecued meat or poultry dishes. Use as a filling for burritos or sopaipillas, or serve alone with a flour tortilla.

Note: This recipe requires advance preparation.

Serves: 6 to 8
Heat Scale: Medium

〰〰〰〰〰〰

SOUTHWESTERN CHIPOTLE-BAKED BEANS

Pinto beans are not the only variety served in the Southwest. Try these interesting great northern beans as a spicy side dish.

JALAPEÑO-CHEDDAR BLUE CORN BREAD

Once you've tasted this recipe, you'll never make bland corn bread again. Adjust the heat upward by doubling the jalapeños, serve it with Original San Antonio Chili (see recipe, p. 66), and your guests will grovel at your feet. If blue cornmeal is not available, substitute the yellow variety.

1	cup coarse blue cornmeal	1½	cups buttermilk
1	cup all-purpose flour	¼	cup finely chopped jalapeño chiles, stems removed
2	teaspoons sugar		
1	teaspoon baking soda	1	cup minced onion
1	teaspoon baking powder	2	eggs, beaten
1	teaspoon salt	1	cup grated cheddar cheese
¼	teaspoon garlic powder		

Combine all the dry ingredients in a bowl.

Heat the buttermilk with the jalapeños and onion for 3 minutes and then allow to cool. Combine the eggs and cheese in another bowl.

Add the milk and egg mixtures to the dry ingredients and blend until smooth.

Pour the batter into a greased 9-inch-square pan and bake in a 350-degree oven for 40 to 50 minutes or until the corn bread is firm and browned.

Serves: 6
Heat Scale: Medium

INDIAN FRY BREAD WITH NO CHILES

Also known as Navajo fry bread, this unique bread is common on the Navajo reservation and among the pueblos along the Rio Grande. It is cooked over piñon wood fires and sold from roadside stands. You can easily re-create the cooking technique in your kitchen.

3 cups flour	1⅓ cups warm water
1½ teaspoons baking powder	vegetable oil for frying
½ teaspoon salt	

Mix the flour, baking powder, and salt together.

Add the water and knead the dough until soft.

Roll the dough out to ¼ inch thick and then cut into rounds 4 to 5 inches in diameter. Poke a small hole in the center of the dough, which will release some of the steam that results from frying.

Fry the dough in 2 to 3 inches of 375-degree oil until puffed and browned on both sides. Drain on paper towels and serve.

Yield: 6 to 8 pieces

~~~~~~~~~~~~~~~~~~~

TRADITIONAL NEW MEXICO
SOPAIPILLAS

In the early days, these "little pillows" were usually served as a bread with New Mexican meals and garnished with honey. Nowadays, home chefs stuff them with meat, beans, cheese, or chiles, alone or in combination.

4 cups all-purpose flour	4 tablespoons shortening
2 teaspoons baking powder	1½ cups warm water
1 teaspoon salt	vegetable oil for frying

Combine all the dry ingredients and cut in the shortening.

Add the water to form a dough and knead it until smooth. Cover and let sit for 30 minutes.

Roll the dough out to ⅛ inch thick and cut into 4-inch squares. Fry the sopaipillas in 375-degree oil until puffed and browned on both sides, about 15 minutes. Drain on paper towels and serve.

Serving Suggestions: Serve with honey, dusted with cinnamon and sugar as a dessert; or stuff with a favorite filling and serve as an entree.

Yield: 4 dozen

BLUE CORN CHILE-BACON MUFFINS

These muffins need not be served at breakfast only. They complement almost any chile dish, barbecue, or Tex-Mex meal.

1 cup flour
¾ cup blue cornmeal
⅓ cup sugar
3 teaspoons baking powder
¾ teaspoon salt
1 cup milk

1 egg, beaten
2 tablespoons melted butter
3 strips crisply cooked bacon, crumbled
4 jalapeños, stems and seeds removed, chopped

Mix the dry ingredients together.

Combine the milk, egg, butter, bacon, and jalapeños. Add to the dry ingredients and stir to mix.

Pour into a lightly greased muffin pan and bake in a 425-degree oven for 15 to 20 minutes.

Yield: 12 to 15 muffins
Heat Scale: Medium

CHILE-DUSTED CHEESE *BOLILLOS*

We first tasted the heavenly *bolillo* rolls in Juárez, where they are stuffed with ham and avocados for tortas. Here is our spiced up version.

1	package dry yeast	1	cup grated cheddar cheese
2	cups very warm water	1	tablespoon cumin seeds
1	tablespoon sugar		shortening
2	teaspoons salt	1	egg white, unbeaten
5½	cups sifted flour	1	tablespoon ground red chile

Pour the yeast into the water and stir until dissolved. Allow to sit for 5 minutes.

Add the sugar, salt, and 3 cups of flour and beat until smooth and shiny. Add the cheese and cumin seeds. Stir in 2 cups more flour. Sprinkle the remaining flour on a board and knead the dough, adding more flour if necessary, until it is smooth and shiny (about 5 to 7 minutes). Shape into a ball.

Rub a bowl lightly with shortening and press the ball of dough into the bowl, then turn the dough over. Cover with a warm, damp towel. Place in a draft-free area and allow to rise until doubled, about 2 hours.

Punch the dough down and let rest for 5 minutes. Rub a little shortening on your hands and divide the dough into 6 equal portions. To form a roll, shape each portion into an oblong and place on a lightly greased sheet pan. Make two horizontal indentations on each roll and bake in a 375-degree oven for 30 minutes or until lightly browned.

Brush each roll with the egg white, sprinkle with the ground chile, and return to the oven for 2 minutes. Remove and cool.

Yield: 6
Heat Scale: Mild

SPICY PUMPKIN ROLLS

Try serving these spicy pumpkin and orange rolls with your next turkey dinner or at breakfast in place of a less nutritious sweet roll.

⅔ cup milk
1   cup cooked mashed pumpkin
⅓ cup brown sugar
2   tablespoons orange zest
2   tablespoons ground red New
    Mexican chile

½   teaspoon salt
⅓ cup butter or margarine
1   package yeast dissolved in
     ¼ cup warm water
4–5 cups whole wheat flour
1   cup raisins

Scald the milk and allow to cool.

Combine the pumpkin, sugar, orange zest, ground chile, salt, and butter and mix well.

Add the yeast mixture and 2 cups of flour and beat well. Gradually stir in the raisins and more flour until the dough is stiff enough to be kneaded. Knead on a floured board until the dough is smooth and elastic.

Place in a buttered bowl, cover, and let rise until doubled in size.

Punch down and turn onto a floured board. Divide into 12 portions and place in a buttered muffin tin. Cover and let rise until doubled.

Bake in a 400-degree oven for 20 minutes. Brush with soft butter while hot.

Yield: 12
Heat Scale: Mild

GUACAMOLE BREAD

This bread has all the makings for the famous appetizer baked right into it. Serve it plain or use it in a sandwich for a unique Southwestern taste.

2 tablespoons chopped onion	1 cup sugar
1 tablespoon butter or margarine	1 cup mashed avocado
2 cups flour	2 eggs, beaten
1½ teaspoons baking powder	3 green New Mexican chiles, roasted, peeled, stems and seeds removed, chopped
½ teaspoon salt	
¼ teaspoon ground cumin	
½ cup butter or margarine, softened	

Saute the onion in the tablespoon of butter until softened.

Sift together all the dry ingredients.

Cream together the softened butter and sugar. Add the avocado, eggs, onion, and chiles.

Add the dry ingredients to the avocado mixture and mix well.

Pour the batter into a buttered 9-by-5–inch loaf pan and bake for 15 minutes at 375 degrees. Reduce heat to 350 degrees and continue to cook for 55 minutes or until done.

Yield: 1 loaf
Heat Scale: Mild

Desert Desserts

The finest complement to heat is sweet. For dousing the fire of hot foods, the combination of sugar, dairy products, and fruits just can't be beat. Here are our favorite Southwestern cooldown desserts, including one with chile!

NEW MEXICAN HOT CHOCOLATE
WITH CINNAMON

This chocolate drink is not only a great way to start the day, it's also a fine way to end a meal or to warm body and soul on a cold winter night.

2 squares sweet chocolate	2 tablespoons ground instant coffee
½ cup boiling water	
1 quart whole or low-fat milk	½ teaspoon vanilla
1 cinnamon stick, 1 inch long	½ teaspoon ground nutmeg

In a pan, dissolve the chocolate in the boiling water.

In another pan, heat the milk, cinnamon, and coffee to the boiling point, then remove from heat. Strain the milk mixture and add it to the dissolved chocolate. Heat to the boiling point and then remove from the heat.

Add the vanilla and nutmeg and beat until foamy with an egg beater or a *molinillo*, a low-tech but efficient Mexican chocolate beater. Serve immediately.

Yield: 1 quart

THE HONORABLE BISCOCHITO FROM
THE LAND OF ENCHANTMENT

These cookies are so distinctly New Mexican that despite the fact that they were copied directly from Old Mexican *biscochitos*, they have been named the New Mexico State Cookie. By the way, they are at their delicious best when served with Citrus Sorbet (see recipe, p. 154).

1	pound soft butter	3	teaspoons baking powder
1½	cups sugar	1	teaspoon salt
2	teaspoons anise seeds	½	cup brandy
2	eggs, beaten	¼	cup sugar
6	cups flour	1	tablespoon ground cinnamon

Cream together the first three ingredients. Add the eggs and beat well.

Mix the flour, baking powder, and salt and sift together three times.

Add the flour mixture 1 cup at a time to the creamed butter, mixing well after each addition.

Pour the brandy over the dough, mix well, and knead lightly to hold the dough together.

Combine the sugar and cinnamon in a separate bowl.

Roll the dough out ¼ inch thick and cut into fancy shapes, such as chiles, coyotes, or saguaro cacti.

Dip each cookie in the cinnamon sugar and then bake on a cookie sheet at 350 degrees for 10 to 12 minutes or until golden brown.

Yield: 4 to 5 dozen

HUEVOS REALES CON PIÑONES

These ''royal eggs'' are an elegant, tasty dessert that never fails to intrigue guests.

8	egg yolks	¼	cup sherry, rum, or brandy
1	cup sugar	5	tablespoons coarsely chopped raisins
3	cloves	5	tablespoons chopped piñon nuts
½	teaspoon cinnamon		
½	cup water		

Puree the egg yolks in a blender until thick, then pour into a buttered baking dish. Set the baking dish inside another, larger baking dish full of water and bake at 350 degrees until the eggs are puffy, about 30 minutes.

Combine the sugar, cloves, and cinnamon with the water and boil for five minutes. Discard the cloves and add the liquor. Set the syrup aside.

Cut the baked eggs into triangles and soak them in the syrup for at least 2 hours. Top the egg triangles with the raisins and piñons and serve.

Note: This recipe requires advance preparation.

Serves: 6

~~~~~~~~~~~~~~~~~

CITRUS SORBET WITH TOASTED PECANS

Sorbets are fruit juices or pureed fruits mixed with syrup and frozen. They are easy to make and very, very refreshing on a hot summer day or as a light ending to a spicy meal. They are often used in expensive restaurants to "clear the palate" between courses, whatever that means.

2 cups sugar
1 cup water
1 cup fresh orange juice
1 cup fresh grapefruit juice

¼ cup fresh lime juice
grated peel of 1 orange
toasted pecan pieces for garnish

Combine the sugar and water and heat until the sugar dissolves. Increase the heat and boil the syrup for 30 seconds. Allow the mixture to cool completely before using.

Combine the cooled syrup with the rest of the ingredients, except the pecans, and process in an ice cream maker according to the directions. Freeze until firm.

To serve, scoop the sorbet into individual bowls and garnish with the toasted pecans.

Serves: 6

NATILLAS WITH BRANDY
AND CHOCOLATE

This soft custard pudding is also called Spanish Cream. It is one of the easier desserts to prepare, and the cook has the enjoyable task of selecting the commercial chocolate bar for the garnish.

4	eggs, separated	¼	teaspoon ground cinnamon
4	tablespoons flour	1	tablespoon brandy
4	cups whole milk	1	milk chocolate candy bar, shaved*
¾	cup sugar		
¼	teaspoon ground nutmeg		

Combine the egg yolks, flour, and 1 cup of the milk and beat to form a smooth paste.

Combine the remaining milk and sugar and heat to scalding. Add the egg mixture and continue to cook on medium heat until thickened to a soft custard consistency. Remove from the heat, allow to cool, and stir in the nutmeg, cinnamon, and brandy.

Beat the egg whites until they are stiff but not dry. Gently fold them into the custard and dish into individual serving bowls. Chill and garnish with the shaved chocolate before serving.

Serves: 6 to 8

*To shave chocolate, chill the chocolate bar. Using a vegetable peeler, shave or peel long, micro-thin ''curls'' off the bar. The bar must be nearly frozen to achieve the best results.

PUMPKIN FLAN WITH CARAMEL SAUCE

Flan is a traditional Mexican custard dessert that has been adopted by all parts of the Southwest. This version is flavored with another favorite north-of-the-border taste, pumpkin.

⅔	cup water	1	teaspoon each ground cinnamon, nutmeg, ginger
2	cups sugar		
3½	cups whole milk	1	tablespoon dark rum
1	vanilla bean	1	cup canned pumpkin
6	eggs		

Place the water and 1 cup of the sugar in a heavy saucepan. Over low heat, stir until the sugar dissolves. Increase the heat and boil until the mixture is light brown. Reduce the heat and simmer until the syrup is an amber color, swirling the pan occasionally to push any crystals back into the syrup. Allow to cool slightly, then pour evenly into 6 warmed custard cups so that the caramel syrup coats them.

Scald the milk and vanilla bean. Remove from the heat and allow to cool. Remove the vanilla bean.

Beat the eggs, spices, and rum together until foamy. Whisk in the remaining sugar and the pumpkin. Gradually add the scalded milk, stirring until the sugar dissolves.

Pour the mixture into the custard cups. Place the cups in a pan with enough hot water to come halfway up the sides of the cups.

Bake in a 350-degree oven for 60 to 70 minutes or until a thin knife inserted halfway between the center and the edge of the custard comes out clean.

Run a thin knife around the edge of the cup and invert the custard onto a dish. Before serving, let the custard sit at room temperature for 10 minutes to set. You can also prepare the flan ahead, chill, and serve.

Serves: 6

WILD BLACKBERRY EMPANADITAS

Curiously, *empanada* means both "pie" and "swindle" in Spanish, so we supposed that these little stuffed pies are so good that people will steal for them. Dessert empanaditas can be filled with almost any type of fruit; traditionally, they are made with a mixture of meat, fruit, and nuts.

THE FILLING

2 cups wild blackberries or other fruits such as strawberries, apricots, apples, or peaches
1 cup water
½ cup raisins

½ cup sugar
1 teaspoon grated lemon peel
½ teaspoon cinnamon
¼ teaspoon cloves

Combine the fruit and 1 cup of water in a saucepan and cook over low heat until the mixture mounds on a spoon, adding more water if needed.

Add the remaining ingredients and stir until the sugar dissolves. Allow to cool.

THE PASTRY

2 cups flour
2 teaspoons baking powder
½ teaspoon salt
⅓ cup shortening

⅓ cup cold water
1 egg, beaten
sugar

Sift the dry ingredients together.

With a pastry blender, cut in the shortening until the flour resembles fine crumbs. Add just enough water so that the dough holds together. Chill for an hour.

Roll the dough out ⅛ inch thick and cut into circles 3 inches in diameter.

Place 1 tablespoon of the filling on half of each circle. Moisten the edges with water, fold over, and crimp with a fork to seal.

Brush the top of each empanadita with the egg, sprinkle with sugar, and bake in a 400-degree oven for 15 minutes or until golden brown. Or omit the egg and sugar and deep-fry in 375-degree oil until golden brown. Remove and drain on paper towels.

Yield: 20 to 24 pastries

BLUE CORNMEAL CREPES
WITH TWO CHEESES

Here is the Southwestern version of dessert crepes, complete with blue corn for that wonderfully exotic color. Again, if blue corn flour is not available, substitute the yellow variety.

THE FILLING

¼ cup cream cheese	2 tablespoons sugar
¼ cup ricotta cheese	1 tablespoon Amaretto liqueur
¼ cup heavy cream	¼ teaspoon almond extract

Allow all the ingredients to come to room temperature and mix together.

THE CREPES

1 egg, beaten	3 tablespoons Amaretto liqueur
¾ cup milk	½ cup blue corn flour
1 tablespoon butter or	powdered sugar
margarine, melted	

Slowly whisk the liquid ingredients into the flour. Cover and let stand at room temperature for an hour.

Lightly oil a crepe or nonstick pan and heat until almost smoking.

Pour 2 tablespoons of the batter into the pan and gently tilt the pan to thinly spread the batter. Cook until the crepe turns light brown on the edges, about 1 minute. Flip and cook the crepe on the other side.

Place 2 tablespoons of the filling in each crepe. Roll up, dust with powdered sugar, and serve.

Serves: 4

SOUTHWESTERN PINEAPPLE CAKE

Pineapples were named by early Spanish explorers in Mexico because the fruit resembles a pine cone. *Apple* was a generic word for fruit in those days. This cake is delicious and easy to make.

THE CAKE

1 20-ounce can crushed pineapple, not drained	2 teaspoons baking soda
2 cups flour	2 cups sugar
1 cup pecans, chopped	2 eggs, beaten

Combine all ingredients and mix well. Pour into a greased 9-by-13–inch baking pan and bake at 350 degrees for 45 minutes.

THE FROSTING

8 ounces cream cheese, softened	1 stick butter, melted
2 cups powdered sugar	1 teaspoon vanilla

Combine all ingredients and mix well. Frost the cake while it is still hot.

Serves: 6

~~~~~~~~~~~~~~~

TAMALES DULCE

Sweet tamales are usually served for dessert. Different fruits can be used. The tamales can also be served unwrapped, topped with a sweet sauce.

1 cup chopped apricots	½ cup sugar
½ cup raisins	2 cups masa harina
½ cup chopped pecans (or other nuts)	½ teaspoon salt
corn husks	1 teaspoon cinnamon
⅓ cup lard or vegetable shortening	1 cup water
	1 teaspoon baking powder

Combine the apricots, raisins, and pecans.

Soak the corn husks in water to soften.

Cream the shortening and sugar together. Mix together the masa harina, salt, and cinnamon. Slowly add the water, stirring with a fork until the mixture holds together. Whip the lard or shortening until fluffy. Add the masa mixture to the shortening and continue to beat. When the dough is the right consistency, beat in the baking powder. Drop a teaspoonful of dough into a glass of cold water. If the masa floats, it is ready. If it sinks, continue to beat it until it floats.

To assemble, select corn husks that measure about 5 by 8 inches or overlap smaller ones together. Place 2 tablespoons of masa in the center of a husk and pat or spread the dough evenly into a 2-by-3–inch rectangle. Place about 2 teaspoons of filling down the center and fold the husk around the masa and filling, being careful not to squeeze the tamale.

There are two basic ways of securing the corn husks. The first is to use two strips of husks to firmly tie each end of the tamale. This method works well with smaller corn husks.

The second method is to fold the tapered end over the filled husk and then fold the remaining end over it. Tie the tamale around the middle with a strip of husk to keep the ends folded down.

Place a rack in the bottom of a steamer or large pot. Make sure that the rack is high enough to keep the tamales above the water. Place the tamales on the rack, folded side down; if the pot is large enough, stand them up. Do not pack them tightly because they need to expand as they cook. Cover with additional husks or a towel to absorb the moisture. Bring the water to a boil, reduce to a gentle boil, and steam for an hour for each dozen tamales or until done. To test for doneness, open one end of the husk; if the masa pulls away from the wrapper, it is done.

Yield: 2 dozen

CALIFORNIA CHOCOLATE CAKE

This cake was served in Southern California around the turn of the century and still holds up today as a delicious dessert. Be sure to use Mexican chocolate, such as Ibarra, which combines cinnamon with chocolate in its round, 3-inch cakes.

THE CAKE

2 cakes Mexican chocolate
½ cup butter
1 cup brown sugar
4 eggs, separated and the whites beaten

1 cup milk
3 cups flour
2 tablespoons baking powder
1 teaspoon vanilla

Melt the chocolate in a saucepan, stir in the butter, brown sugar, and egg yolks, and beat well. Add the remaining ingredients, including the beaten egg whites, and mix thoroughly. Pour into a greased 8-by-8-inch pan and bake at 350 degrees for 40 minutes.

Remove from the oven and allow to cool. Remove from pan.

THE ICING

1 cake Mexican chocolate
1 tablespoon butter

½ cup brown sugar

Mix all ingredients together in a double boiler and heat until thick, stirring occasionally with a whisk. Remove from the heat and cool. Spread the icing over the cake. Allow to cool for a few minutes before serving.

Serves: 6

WEDDING COOKIES

Commonly served at celebrations in the Southwest, these cookies are simple and quick to prepare.

1 cup butter or margarine, softened
½ cup confectioners' sugar
1 teaspoon vanilla extract
2 cups flour

¼ teaspoon salt
1 cup ground pecans or walnuts
confectioners' sugar

Cream the first 2 ingredients. Beat in the vanilla.

Sift the flour and salt together. Beat the flour mixture into the butter mixture. Add the nuts and continue to beat until the dough holds together.

Form into 1- to 1½-inch balls. Bake at 350 degrees on ungreased baking sheets for 12 to 15 minutes or until lightly browned.

Remove and cool slightly, then roll in confectioners' sugar while still warm.

Yield: 4 dozen cookies

CHILE FRUIT SUNDAE

The combination of fruit and chile is quite common in Mexico, where you can purchase fresh fruit dusted with ground red chile from street vendors. The mix of hot and sweet provides a refreshing end to any meal.

3 tablespoons cider vinegar	1 cup cubed watermelon
2 tablespoons sugar	1 cup cubed fresh pineapple
¼ teaspoon crushed Habanero chile	1 cup sliced fresh strawberries

Heat the vinegar and sugar until the sugar dissolves. Stir in the chile and allow to cool. Pour over the fruit and chill until time to serve.

Serves: 4
Heat Scale: Hot

MAIL ORDER SOURCES
FOR SOUTHWESTERN COOKING

Seeds

Native Seeds/SEARCH
2509 North Campbell Avenue,
  #325
Tucson, AZ 85719
(602) 327-9123

Plants of the Southwest
Route 6, Box 11-A
Santa Fe, NM 87501
(505) 438-8888

Seeds of Change
1364 Rufina Circle
Santa Fe, NM 87501
(505) 983-8956

Seeds West
P.O. Box 1739
El Prado, NM 87529
(505) 758-7268

Shepherd's Garden Seeds
Shipping Office
30 Irene Street
Torrington, CT 06790
(203) 482-3638

Cookbooks and Publications

Chile Pepper **Magazine**
P.O. Box 4278
Albuquerque, NM 87196
(800) 359-1483

Jessica's Biscuit
P.O. Box 301
Newtonville, MA 02160
(800) 878-4264

Out West Publishing
P.O. Box 4278
Albuquerque, NM 87196
(800) 359-1483

Food and Gifts

Casados Farms
P.O. Box 1269
San Juan Pueblo, NM 87566
(505) 852-2433

Chile Pepper Emporium
328 San Felipe Road NW
Albuquerque, NM 87104
(505) 242-7538

Eagle Ranch Pistachio Groves
Route 1, Box 257
Alamogordo, NM 88310
(800) 432-0999

Fredericksburg Herb Farm
P.O. Drawer 927
Fredericksburg, TX 78624
(800) 284-0525

Hobson Gardens
Route 2, 3656 East Hobson
 Road
Roswell, NM 88201
(800) 488-7298

New Mexican Connection
2833 Rhode Island NE
Albuquerque, NM 87110
(505) 292-5493

New Mexico Catalog
P.O. Box 261
Fairacres, NM 88033
(800) 678-0585

**Old Southwest Trading
Company**
P.O. Box 7545
Albuquerque, NM 87194
(505) 836-0168

Pendery's Spices
304 East Belknap
Fort Worth, TX 76102
(800) 533-1870

Santa Fe Exotix
Route 9, Box 56C
Santa Fe, NM 87501
(505) 988-7063

Simply Southwest by Mail
7404 Menaul NE
Albuquerque, NM 87110
(800) 447-6177

Southwest America
1506-C Wyoming NE
Albuquerque, NM 87112
(505) 299-1856

**Southwestern Flavor
Company**
P.O. Box 315
Red River, NM 87558
(505) 754-2221

**Stonewall Chile Pepper
Company**
P.O. Box 241
Stonewall, TX 78671
(800) 232-2995

GLOSSARY OF SOUTHWESTERN COOKING TERMS AND INGREDIENTS

Achiote The orange-colored seed of the annatto tree; used as a coloring agent and seasoning.

Adobado In Texas, a sour marinade paste made with herbs, chiles, and vinegar. In New Mexico and El Paso, a marinade for pork made with New Mexican red chiles, garlic, and oregano (called *adovada*).

Adobo A thick cooking sauce comprised of tomatoes, vinegar, and spices.

Adovada See *adobado*.

Agua fresca A drink made with fresh fruit.

Ajo Garlic.

Albóndiga Meatball.

Al carbón Grilled over charcoal.

Al pastór Cooked on a spit over a fire.

Anaheim chile A misnomer for the New Mexican chile; now the term for a very mild New Mexican cultivar grown only in California.

Ancho chile The dried form of the poblano chile. Substitute pasilla chiles.

Antojito Literally, "little whim"; an appetizer.

Arroz Rice.

Asada Roasted or broiled (also called *asado*).

Asadero A type of rubbery white cheese at first made only in the Mexican states of Chihuahua and Michoacán but now produced in the United States as well. Substitute Monterey Jack.

Azafran Saffron.

Barbacoa In Texas, pit-barbecued meat; in Mexico, the barbecued flesh of a cow's head.

Biscochito In New Mexico, an anise-flavored cookie (called *bizcochito* in Mexico).

Blue corn   A variety of corn with blue kernels, which are ground into blue cornmeal and blue corn flour.

Bolillo   A Mexican hard roll; similar to french bread.

Borracho   Literally, "drunken"; applied to food containing beer or liquor.

Burrito   In New Mexico and Texas, a flour tortilla stuffed with combinations of meat, cheese, beans, chile sauce, and other ingredients; called "burro" in Arizona.

Burro   See *burrito.*

Cabrito   Roasted kid (young goat, that is).

Calabacita   Squash, usually zucchini types.

Calamari   Squid.

Caldillo   Literally, "little soup"; a thick stew with beef and chiles, commonly served in El Paso and Juárez.

Caldo   A broth, stock, or clear soup.

Canela   Cinnamon.

Capriotada   A bread pudding dessert.

Carne   Meat.

Carnitas   Literally, "little pieces of meat"; small chunks of pork fried to a crisp texture.

Cascabel chile   Literally, "jingle bell"; a small round hot chile that rattles when shaken. Substitute chiles de árbol.

Ceviche   Raw seafood combined with lime juice, which "cooks" the fish by combining with its protein and turning it opaque.

Chalupa   Literally, "little boat"; in New Mexico, a fried corn tortilla in the shape of a boat containing shredded chicken or beans topped with salsa, guacamole, or cheese.

Chayote   A pear-shaped member of the squash family primarily grown in Mexico.

Chicharrón   Crisp-fried pork skin.

Chicos   Roasted and dried kernels of corn.

Chilaquiles   A casserole made of tortilla wedges, salsa, and cheese.

Chile   The plant or pod of the genus *Capsicum.*

Chile caribe   A red chile paste made from garlic, water, and crushed or ground red chiles of any type.

Chile con queso   A cheese and chile dip.

Chile de árbol   A hot dried red chile from Mexico. Substitute dried red New Mexican chiles or chiltepíns.

Chile pasado   Literally, ''chile of the past''; a roasted, peeled, and sun-dried New Mexican or poblano chile.

Chili   Chile sauce with meat; chili con carne.

Chilipiquín   See *Chiltepín chile.*

Chiltepín chile   A round hot chile the size of a peppercorn that grows wild in Arizona. A wild Texas variety is called ''chilipiquín'' (also ''chile pequín,'' ''chili tepín''). Substitute ground cayenne or hot red ground chile.

Chimichanga   A deep-fried, stuffed burro topped with cheese and chile sauce.

Chipotle chile   A smoked and dried jalapeño. Substitute *moritas* (smoked serranos).

Chorizo   A spicy sausage made with pork, garlic, and ground red chile.

Cilantro   An annual herb (*Coriandrum sativum*) with seeds (which are known as ''coriander''). Substitute Italian parsley or culantro (*Eryngium foetidum*). Commonly used in salsas and soups.

Comal   Griddle.

Comino   See *cumin.*

Coriander   See *cilantro.*

Cumin   An annual herb (*Cuminum cyminum*) whose seeds have a distinctive odor; the dominant flavor in Tex-Mex dishes like chili con carne.

Desayuno   Breakfast.

Empanadita   A pastry turnover.

Enchilada   A rolled tortilla or a stack of tortillas filled with meat or cheese and covered with chile sauce.

Epazote   Known as ''ambrosia'' in English, this perennial herb (*Chenopodium ambrosioides*) is strong and bitter and is primarily used to flavor beans.

Escabeche   Vegetables, especially chiles, marinated or pickled in vinegar.

Fajita   Literally, ''little belt''; marinated and grilled skirt steak.

Flan   A baked caramel custard dessert.

Flauta   Literally, ''flute''; a tightly rolled, deep-fried stuffed tortilla.

Frijoles   Beans.

Gordita   Literally, "little fat one"; a stuffed corn cake.

Guacamole   Literally, "mixture of vegetables"; in this case, a blend of avocados, tomatoes, garlic, and chiles.

Habanero chile   Literally, "from Havana"; a small orange or red chile from the Caribbean and Yucatán that resembles a tam or bonnet; the hottest in the world. Substitute jalapeños or serranos.

Hongo   Mushroom.

Huevos rancheros   Literally, "ranch-style eggs."

Jalapeño chile   A small hot fat chile; it is pickled, stuffed, or used fresh in salsas. Substitute serranos.

Jamaica   A Mexican flower that flavors teas and other beverages.

Jamón   Ham.

Jicama   A white tuber (*Pachyrhizus erosus*) used in salads; it tastes like a cross between an apple and a potato.

Langosta   Lobster.

Lengua   Tongue.

Lima   Lemon.

Limón   Lime.

Machaca   Stewed, roasted, or broiled meat that is shredded.

Maíz   Corn.

Manteca   Lard or butter.

Masa   Corn flour dough.

Masa harina   Corn flour.

Menudo   Tripe soup, often with chiles.

Mescal   A liquor distilled from the agave plant.

Metate   A stone for grinding corn.

Mexican oregano   A shrub (*Lippia graveolens*) of southern Mexico that differs from European oregano (*Origanum vulgare*), whose true name is wild marjoram.

Migas   In Texas, eggs scrambled with chorizo, tortilla chips, onions, tomatoes, cheese, and serrano chiles.

Mirasol chile   A small hot red chile from Mexico. The name in Spanish means "looking at the sun," an allusion to the upright pods on the plant.

Molcajete   A mortar made out of volcanic stone.

Mole   Literally, "mixture"; usually refers to a thick chile sauce made with chocolate and many spices.

Molinillo   A wooden beater used in the preparation of hot chocolate.

Morita chile   A smoke-dried serrano chile.

Nachos   Tostadas topped with cheese and sliced jalapeños.

Natilla   A custard dessert.

New Mexican chile   The "long green" chile grown in New Mexico; varieties include Big Jim, No. 6-4, Sandia, Española, and Chimayó, ranging in heat from mild to medium. Substitute poblanos.

Nopal   The pad of the prickly pear cactus, spines removed; also called *nopalito.*

Nopalito   See *nopal.*

Olla   A round, earthenware pot.

Pan   Bread; sweet bread is called *pan dulce.*

Papa   Potato.

Parrilla   Grill or broiler.

Pasilla chile   Literally, "little raisin," an illusion to the aroma and dark brown color of this long thin mild Mexican chile. Substitute anchos.

Pepitas   Roasted pumpkin seeds.

Pescado   Fish.

Picadillo   Shredded beef, spices, and other ingredients usually used as a stuffing.

Picante   Hot and spicy.

Pico de gallo   Literally, "beak of the rooster"; a salsa with tomatoes, onions, cilantro, and serrano chiles.

Piloncillo   Brown, unrefined cane sugar.

Piñon   The nut of the piñon tree (*Pinus edulis*). Substitute pine nuts.

Pipian   A sauce containing spices and ground nuts or seeds.

Poblano chile   Literally, "pepper of the people"; this dark-green, fat, mild chile is commonly used in Mexico and the Southwest. Substitute fresh New Mexicans. The dried form is called *ancho,* "wide."

Pollo   Chicken.

Posole   A thick stew made with pork, chiles, and hominy corn.

Posole corn   A limed corn (hominy), available either dried or frozen.

Puerco   Pork.

Quelites   A spinach and bean dish seasoned with chile and bacon.

Quesadilla   A flour tortilla turnover, usually stuffed with cheese, then toasted, fried, or baked.

Queso Cheese.

Raja A strip; usually refers to a strip of chiles.

Ranchero Ranch-style.

Refrito Refried; used mainly to describe beans that are mashed and fried in lard.

Relleno Stuffed.

Res Beef.

Ristra A string of red chile pods.

Rocoto chile A small, apple-shaped, hot chile with black seeds. Originally from South America, it is grown in mountainous regions of Mexico.

Saguaro A tall cactus found in Arizona; its fruit is made into jams and jellies.

Salpicón A Mexican shredded-meat salad.

Salsa Literally, ''sauce,'' but usually used to describe uncooked sauces (salsa cruda).

Serrano chile A small hot Mexican chile, usually pickled or used green or red in fresh salsas. Substitute jalapeños.

Sopa Soup.

Sopaipilla From *sopaipa,* a fritter soaked in honey; in New Mexico, a puffed, fried bread served with honey or filled with various stuffings.

Taco A stuffed corn tortilla, either soft or crisp.

Taquito A rolled, deep-fried taco.

Tamale Any filling enclosed in masa, wrapped in corn husks, and steamed.

Tamarindo Tamarind.

Tequila A type of mescal produced near Tequila in the state of Jalisco, Mexico.

Tomatillo A small green husk tomato (*Physalis ixocarpa*). Substitute small regular tomatoes.

Torta A sandwich, often made with a bolillo.

Tostada A tortilla chip.

Tuna The fruit of the prickly pear cactus.

Yerba buena Mint.

INDEX

Poultry. *See also* Chicken; Game hens
  quail with goat cheese rounds, grape
    grilled, 100–101
  smoked turkey with cascabel oil, 94
Prawns. *See* Shrimp
Prickly pears, 9
  chile cactus salad, 36–37
Pueblo chile fritters, 139
Pueblo Indians, 4
Pumpkin
  flan with caramel sauce, 156
  rolls, spicy, 149
  ¡Ole Mole sauce!, seeds in, 49

Q
Quail with goat cheese rounds, grape
    grilled, 100–101
Quesadillas with goat cheese, 17
Queso flameado with poblano strips,
    24–25
Quiche macho-style, 118–119

R
Raisins
  mesquite-grilled chicken with apple
    pistachio chutney, 96
  molletes de calabaza, 149
  ¡Ole Mole sauce!, 49
  tamales dulce, 159–160
Rajas
  marinated, 19–20
Ramsdell, Charles, 7
Red snapper
  mesquite-grilled snapper with ancho
    sauce, 106–107
  seafood flautas, 109
Ribs barbecued Texas-style, 84
Rice
  corn and jalapeño custard, 132
  green and hot, 143–144
  Southwestern spicy pork paella with
    artichokes, 80
  tomatillo and habanero rice, 144
Ricotta cheese
  blue cornmeal crepes with two
    cheeses, 158

lasagna, Southwestern, 124
  roasted poblano chiles with spiced
    goat cheese, 122
Roasted corn and crab bisque, 63
Roasted poblano chiles with spiced
    goat cheese, 122
Roasted saguaro jam-glazed game hens
    with corn bread, piñon and green
    chile stuffing, 90
Roasted serrano and tomato salsa, 43
Roasting and peeling chiles, 11–12
Rolls
  chile-dusted cheese bolillos, 148
  molletes de calabaza, 149
Route 66 soup, 62
Routh Street Cafe, 11

S
Sagahún, Bernardino de, 2
Saguaro fruits, 9
St. Estephe Restaurant, 10
Salads. *See also* Dressings
  avocado mousse, 31–32
  in California cuisine, 10
  chile cactus salad, 36–37
  hot wilted spinach salad, 34–35
  marinated vegetables with sun-dried
    tomatoes, 38
  salpicón, 33
  Santa Fe greens with green chile
    mayonnaise, 28
  Sonoran-style taco salad, 30–31
  Southwestern Crab Louis, 32–33
  Spanish California ripe olive salad,
    35–36
  stir-fry pork and avocado salad,
    37
  Texas caviar, 34
  Tex-Mex coleslaw for the barbecue,
    29
Salmon in seafood flautas, 109
Salpicón, 33
Salsa borracha herradura, 41–42
Salsa cruda, 40
Salsa fresca, 40